TITANIC
BEHIND THE SCENES

Exploring Why the Titanic Continues to Fascinate More than a Century After Its Untimely Demise

Campbell Cloar

ISBN: 9781796537369

Cover design by Amy AP Designworks LLC

Would you like to know the surprising answers to the top five questions people ask about the *Titanic at Titanic Museum Attraction*, where I work? I've written these in a short booklet and would love to get them to you. Find this free offer at ShipsLogTitanic.com.

The Titanic Pigeon Forge Crew arranged on the Grand Staircase in May, 2018. At the front right is Mary Kellogg-Joslyn who, with husband John Joslyn, opened *Titanic Museum Attraction* Pigeon Forge in 2010. John and Mary's first *Titanic Museum Attraction* opened in Branson, MO in 2006. Here, Mary is standing beside Vice President of Operations for Cedar Bay Entertainment, Danita Brown.

Contents

About Campbell Cloar

Campbell Cloar is an Original Crew Member at *Titanic Museum Attraction* in Pigeon Forge, TN. That means that he was among the Crew Members who began when the museum opened in 2010.

Prior to joining *Titanic Museum Attraction*, Campbell had careers in broadcasting and teaching.

"I had always been fascinated with radio and television," he says. "My Aunt Lois enjoyed telling a story about when I visited them when I was ten or eleven. A neighbor across the street from their home in Indianapolis phoned to ask Aunt Lois about the little boy who appeared to be talking into the brass coupling at the end of one of those long, green garden hoses."

Campbell smiles as he remembers that story.

"The neighbor asked delicately whether I was alright. She must have thought I was a little strange, talking into a garden hose. But I was pretending to be Bill Cullen, the host of *The Price is Right* back in the 1950's."

Campbell began his career in broadcasting while at Carson-Newman College (now Carson-Newman

University), beginning as a disc jockey when they played vinyl records and played jingles and commercials recorded on eight-track carts. His passion for broadcasting eventually led to a career as a broadcast journalist, which he pursued simultaneously with various teaching assignments.

He earned a Master of Arts in Literature and Writing at Iowa State University, Master of Arts in Teaching at East Tennessee State University, Doctor of Jurisprudence, and Ed.S in Education at the University of Tennessee, Knoxville.

His main passions have always been writing and communications, and he has a special love for the stage and acting.

He and his wife, Imogene, whom he met in his Sophomore year at Carson-Newman, raised three children: Alice, Nick, and Erin. Now they are delighted with their first grandchildren, Lillie and Marina, pictured here with Campbell and Imogene.

A major theme of *Titanic Behind the Scenes* examines one of our main connections with passengers and crew who sailed on *Titanic.* In every era, humans are striving to reach for something just beyond themselves. In our own era, just as in 1912 when *Titanic* thrilled the world, this often involves the adventure of new technology.

Campbell hopes to pursue this theme in his future writing, exploring the idea that our reach toward the adventure of new discovery includes an instinctive reach toward the spiritual, though we do not realize it.

To follow Campbell's pursuit of these themes, visit www.shipslogtitanic.com

Dedication

I've never had any doubt that I would dedicate *Titanic Behind the Scenes* to John and Mary, as they are affectionately known to all of us who work with them at *Titanic Museum Attraction.* It is my hope that this book can be a heartfelt expression of my sincere gratitude for the opportunity to be a part of this incredible museum. I certainly want it to be a tribute to John Joslyn and Mary Kellogg Joslyn, whose dedication and standards of excellence inspire each of us every day.

I have been privileged to see first-hand their standards of excellence for the museum. Beyond that, though, I — like all of the Crew who are a part of *Titanic Museum Attraction*— experience a warmth and genuine concern from John and Mary. They are determined to make *Titanic Museum Attraction* a world-class museum for our guests. And they are no less caring in providing an environment for the Crew that inspires, encourages creativity, and reflects genuine care for each individual on the team.

Before working with John Joslyn to create the first of their two *Titanic Museum Attractions*, which opened in Branson, MO in 2006, Mary Kellogg Joslyn was Senior Vice President of Programming and Production for the Walt Disney Studios. Among her most notable shows are *Regis and Kathy Lee*, and *Who Wants to Be a Millionaire*? She signed the check for the first contestant to win a million dollars on that program.

John Joslyn's name was well known in the world of entertainment before he decided to pioneer a television first. In 1986, he put together a six-million- dollar French-American expedition to the recently discovered *Titanic*, more than two miles below the North Atlantic. His team figured out the cutting-edge technology which would allow production of the first ever television show about *Titanic*, which was an astounding accomplishment and a big hit.

I am immensely grateful to John and Mary for allowing me to be a part of *Titanic Museum Attraction.* I'm sure I speak for each Crew Member when I say we are all experiencing something unprecedented. We are beneficiaries of an environment that allows each of us the confidence to excel. What an honor to be a part of a world-class museum that allows our guests to interact with the *Titanic* and its significance for the world of 1912 and for our own era, as well.

John and Mary inspire us—always—to do our very best to give our guests a memorable experience as we encourage them to enter the world of more than a hundred years ago. And what is our central focus? What is the foundation of what John and Mary have always envisioned for these museums?

It is to honor the passengers and crew who sailed the *Titanic.*

As John Joslyn has always said, "We tell their stories."

John and Mary are our role models, and we are better individuals because of the standards they set and the genuine concern they have for each one of us.

So, thank you, John and Mary. May *Titanic Behind the Scenes* be a tribute to your vision and to how you have set the standard for what is possible. *Titanic* is often referred to as the *ship of dreams.* That also applies to the world John and Mary have created at *Titanic Museum Attraction*—an inspiring experience for guests and Crew alike.

Introduction

For me, the opportunity to be part of *Titanic Museum Attraction* began on a Thursday evening in 2009 with a phone call from my daughter, Alice, who is a kitchen designer in Knoxville, TN.

She said, "Hey, I just heard on the news that there is a new museum opening soon in Pigeon Forge. It will be a *Titanic* museum, and they've issued a casting call."

Alice is the oldest of my three children, and growing up with me, all three—Alice, Nick, and Erin—know how I love acting. My wife, Imogene, and I actually met during auditions for Arthur Miller's *The Crucible* at Carson-Newman, the liberal arts college where we earned our undergraduate degrees.

A family story is that the first words my wife ever heard me utter were, "I'll be damned first!" I was so nervous during my audition to be Judge Hawthorne in *The Crucible* that my voice made the rafters shake.

I got the part, though, and later was George Tesman in Ibsen's *Hedda Gabler,* and I was the Handsome Young Man in *My Three Angels,* part of which takes place in Cherbourg, France. Cherbourg was *Titanic's* first stop after setting out from Southampton, England on her maiden voyage. Imogene, also a lover of theater, enchanted audiences in her role as Mariane in Molière's *Tartuffe.*

Perhaps it is no wonder, then, that our kids were raised in an atmosphere of theater at home, where we often launched into spontaneous re-enactments of their favorite childhood books. They also enjoyed a vibrant youth program at church which included skits and plays.

Meanwhile, I was earning a living entertaining on radio and later as a broadcast journalist. I also taught Freshman Composition courses at Walters State Community College. I studied Law at the University of Tennessee, Knoxville, but then was lured back into teaching.

So, yes, Alice encouraged me to send in my résumé. It was one of those occasions where I did something as a matter of routine, and even when a call came from Danita Brown, Vice President of Operations for Cedar Bay Entertainment, I had no idea what an incredible opportunity this would be, or of the impact it would have on my life.

Titanic Behind the Scenes showcases this amazing venue—*Titanic Museum Attraction*—offering behind-the-scenes glimpses of guest experiences and lots of information about *Titanic.*

I began this book as a tribute to museum owners John Joslyn and Mary Kellogg Joslyn. However, *Titanic Behind the Scenes* is also a tribute to the talented Crew who bring *Titanic Museum Attraction* to life for museum guests.

Who is this book for?

Perhaps you have always been fascinated by the *Titanic* and would be interested in a unique way of experiencing this ship. *Titanic Behind the Scenes* will show you how this great ship represents an instinctive drive humans experience in every generation to reach beyond ourselves. As the book discusses the *Titanic* in relation to this drive and evolving human identity, you will find new ideas about the ship and how it relates to who we are as a human species and what we are becoming.

Also, because I am a Crew Member at *Titanic Museum Attraction* in Pigeon Forge, TN, I will include observations of our museum guests, artifacts, and even some behind-the-scenes glimpses of this world-class museum.

Your Tour of *Titanic Museum Attraction*

There are more than four hundred artifacts in the museum. The goal is to focus on a selection of artifacts to project the depth of the *Titanic* disaster in a way that delves more deeply, perhaps, or which goes in new directions.

Recently we were honored to loan artifacts to the Reagan Presidential Library in California. The artifacts we sent there included Madeleine Astor's life jacket and a rare, twenty-seven-hundred-year-old Egyptian talisman which once belonged to Margaret Tobin Brown. Some may know her as the Unsinkable Molly Brown.

However, our most important exploration will involve guests to *Titanic Museum Attraction*, many of whom travel great distances—even from other countries—to visit us. The human element, though, is a crucial part of showing how we are all connected, and how in every era we have much in common.

Several years ago, the *Titanic Museum Attraction* parking lot was crowded with people from our own era who feel that tug when they experience the movie we featured outside in the Pigeon Forge evening. They brought lawn chairs, coolers, and a deep longing for this elusive thing we all feel inside as we reach toward this indefinable something just beyond us.

The *Titanic* movie captures it, and as part of our commemoration of the twentieth anniversary, we showed the movie in an outdoor venue, our parking lot. The audience cheered at familiar, much loved scenes, especially the moments which involve the budding romance between Leonardo DiCaprio and Kate Winslet as Jack and Rose. And the audience jeered whenever the terrible Cal appeared.

I believe that our greatest task as humans is one that lies just beyond us like the flat, shimmering waters of a beach as the tide surges in with that mesmerizing rhythm that has always been its signature. It calls to this something deep within us. *Titanic Behind the Scenes* aims to explore the hope and the longing we feel as we risk the most tantalizing scientific explorations.

Chapter One—Humans Are Connected in Every Era

Dressed in my elegant black silk suit with red ascot tie blossoming from my shirtfront, I seem to be succeeding in holding my audience captive with the story of how I—Col. Archibald Gracie—had to balance on the bottom of a capsized lifeboat on the night of the sinking.

"There were thirty of us balancing on the bottom of capsized Collapsible Lifeboat B. We had to stand like this."

I hold my arms out, hoping to imitate the slanted wings of a penguin.

"And I can tcll you, aftcr a whilc your arms fccl likc lead."

There is something wonderfully captivating about the story, and how the storyteller, and the listeners alike, are transported. And I often feel this connection between us when the audience is there, willing and eager, excited for the opportunity to be drawn in, lifted into another time, and for a few moments we are, each of us, out there in the darkness, in the thirty-two-degree air with this frigid seawater sloshing at our feet.

". . . twenty-eight-degree seawater," I am saying. "Imagine."

And that is when young Alex, who has been expertly flicking one of the newest devices that mesmerize our children today—the intrepid fidget-spinner—suddenly glances up. The fidget-spinner's blurred form spins beneath the nearly imperceptible push of his index finger.

I wonder if this young boy is listening, so absorbed he seems in this modern distraction, one of the symbols of our own youth. There always seems to be something. In every generation, something that identifies one of them as young, nimble, and clever.

But Alex glances up and lifts his left hand, patiently waiting, the fidget spinner continuing to revolve between index finger and thumb of his right hand.

"Ah," I say, in my deep, elegant Col. Gracie voice. "I believe we have a question. Yes?"

"If Collapsible Lifeboat B was capsized, how could it still float?" asks Alex. "How come it didn't sink out from under all of you? Thirty men on top. I mean, it seems impossible."

And in a way, it was. Yes, it was impossible, but then how could a ship of steel float gracefully upon the sea and glide so rapidly through the water? There is much that we take for granted.

But I do have an answer for young Alex and for the others, who shift toward me, just a barely perceptible shift, an added stillness coming over them, their eyes fixed upon me, hoping I have a plausible answer.

"It was an air pocket that had formed beneath the lifeboat," I say. "That was the only thing holding it up."

I go on to relate how Second Officer Charles Lightoller was quite stern with all of us. Of course, I am in that moment Col. Gracie, and therefore I am one of the men balancing on top of the capsized lifeboat. And together, the audience and I ease again into that night, into the cold, the starkness of the alien night, alone upon Collapsible Lifeboat B, unsure if any ship has heard the distress call. But Officer Lightoller makes it very clear that we will have to balance carefully.

"If we don't balance," he said, "the air pocket will collapse, and we will all be in the water."

And Alex, continuing his expert stroking of the fidget-spinner, index finger causing it to whirl and hum, asks his next question. He is not looking at me but at something just beyond me. I assume he is living that night and that each of us now has—through story—transitioned to that night, in the cold, balancing on the overturned lifeboat.

"Well there were plenty of people in that twenty-eight-degree water, right?" asks Alex. "How long can you survive if you're in water like that?"

And that is the dark, sad part of the disaster. You can't survive very long, I tell them. It's hypothermia. Your body goes into shock. It's hard to get your breath. It feels like a thousand knives stabbing you all over. At first, anyway. That's what it feels like at first. But then you get numb, and it's like going to sleep.

"You might have anywhere from ten to forty minutes," I tell Alex and all those gathered with us at the Map. "Depends on your will to live and your body weight."

And that is why, when the ship *Carpathia* arrived, anyone in the water was already gone. Those people did not drown, we say, they froze to death. Nearly fifteen hundred people, all gone. Two-thirds of those on the ship did not survive.

Day to day, though, at our museum, I am aware of this tug we feel deep within us. It is powerful and seems riveted into our very DNA. Something draws us; it calls to us.

Titanic Museum Attraction is as much a reminder of something we feel in every age. The *Titanic* is a symbol of this instinctive drive that urges us in every era to reach for something just beyond our grasp.

The *Titanic* was an incredible advance in technology for its era. It was more than a ship. I believe the powerful hold it had even on people of 1912 is that it called to this tug, this pull. And even today, it is a symbol of this pull we feel, an expression of this instinctive tug that defines us and scratches at something just beneath the surface. In every age, it is there.

Much of what inspires me at *Titanic Museum Attraction* is that I see many of our guests in the throes of this unconscious awareness. Even the children experience it.

Every day, I sense a community among our guests. Something happens. Wherever we humans gather, we have a connection. Just as on the *Titanic*, which was a cross section of society of that era, the same is happening at our museum as all sorts of people are drawn to us. Many of them slip into that learning mode. Scientists advise that our brainwaves change in this contemplative, creative mode we slip into.

Families visit with their children, and we are, in a sense, acknowledging who we are. I doubt that many guests would describe it with the same words. Most would smile politely and mumble about how it is just something to do, or about how they always meant to visit our museum, just to see what is here.

But I sense something more, something that connects us as humans in every age. I will attempt to convey this *something more* here as we explore so much that is related to the *Titanic* and this instinctive drive we have in every age to reach beyond ourselves.

Chapter Two—Titanic: Reaching Toward Our Evolving Identity

Some fourteen thousand Irishmen built the *Titanic* and her sister ship, the *Olympic*. The ships were magnificent—marvels of design and technology. But the Grand Staircase has become symbolic of the elegance provided for First Class passengers. The project of carving by hand all the detail work on all six decks of this staircase took nearly two years to complete.

Just past the façade of the famous *Grapes Pub*, there is a case displaying actual pieces of the Aft Grand—a smaller Grand Staircase toward the rear of the ship. And around the corner, a case displaying some of the tools used by Mr. McCauley, one of dozens of master craftsmen who accomplished the hand carving. Even now, here in our own era, we have similar tools designed for us to curl our fingers around as others have done in nearly every human era on the planet.

It is as though time always includes the surf of progressing generations of humans. In the broadest sense, human progression is the flinging forth of genetic material, not unlike the rhythms of the sea. Always this surf of vulnerable chromosomes, genes, our DNA. Frothy, glittery stuff, so frightening in its ferocity, its stubborn, deadly insistence on casting forward repeatedly with the tenacity and rhythms of the sea. There is the vast, oscillating power of this massive water that has covered most of the planet through every human generation.

The lure of the *Titanic*, a magnificent vessel created to defy the sea, enchants us even now. No doubt it is part of the pull the sea has upon something instinctive within us.

Often, an entire age is defined by some major leap forward. Perhaps it is a work of literature, art, music, or science. Sometimes, an era can produce a genius who creates some breathtaking work or discovery that is transcendent. This work, or a combination of works, propels the human species forward.

The *Titanic* was for the early twentieth century one of these works of genius. A new class of ship, yes. Technologically, it was a wonder. However, there is something much more important. The *Titanic* is one of the expressions of our need to push boundaries, to test ourselves, to reach through exploration toward that aching, instinctive place always calling to us and urging us to leap ahead.

As the twentieth century dawned, citizens sensed that technology was going to be important, exciting, and would propel them into a future of discovery and exhilarating advances in Science.

Titanic was far more than a ship. As magnificent as it was, *Titanic* was more. It was our hopes, our dreams, our evolving identity. *Titanic* implied what we so fiercely wanted to become.

At any moment, parts of the ocean somewhere upon Earth exhibit the savage, wild thunder that has been the bane of these tiny vessels we set bobbing upon the water. Testing our capacities, lured by this inner need to explore, something that is always within us unfurls. It is irrepressible and wild within us. It tempts us and draws our thoughts of what might be out there and what it might be like to rise effortlessly, faces turned upwards. All of us are drawn irresistibly, breathing in that cadence of someone deeply asleep.

The *Titanic* called to that *something* within people of the early twentieth century. The *Titanic* continues to call today, and every year hundreds of thousands visit our Pigeon Forge *Titanic Museum Attraction.* The first *Titanic Museum Attraction* opened in 2006 in Branson, MO.

Our guests often express surprise that our *Titanic Museum Attraction* is landlocked, rising from the Parkway in Pigeon Forge, TN. As I drive toward our ship, as we refer to it, I can look down the Parkway and see the Great Smoky Mountains, like a pack of humpback whales upon the horizon.

And there, near Hatfield and McCoy Dinner Theater and Wonder Works, is the representation of our ship, the *Titanic,* surprising many who have never traveled to this mountain area. As we tell our guests, though, our Attraction is not nearly the size of the actual *Titanic.* It is half-of-half the actual size of the great ship, just enough to lure delighted attention as they drive by. And our ship only has two funnels, rather than *Titanic*'s four. But our ship entices as the long lines of vehicles drive by, many of them headed toward Dollywood and from there into Gatlinburg.

And yes, we are landlocked, surrounded by mountains, but the Great Smoky Mountains National Park is one of the most rapidly visited parks in America, and our owners, Mary Kellogg and John Joslyn, are wise to have placed the museum here.

So many people from so many places glide into this region, as though their vehicles are vessels. Though cars are designed to travel by land and glide upon rubber tires, they are, nevertheless, not unlike the ship platforms we have designed to ride upon the sea. And these land ships we maneuver across our asphalt highways, which are pathways not unlike the channels ships ply in the ocean, are sailing.

As the human species, we create clever crafts, whether these be watercraft or the auto-mobiles that were once the stuff of Jules Verne and science fiction, but which now fill the lanes and asphalt pathways we have rolled out across the planet, always moving like the corpuscles that jiggle and careen through the arteries within us. We have even begun to refer to these asphalt pathways as arteries. This main artery here, we say, connects with that one over there. We have blood vessels within us, and we name our ships vessels, wondrous crafts which ply the sea lanes, which we often think of as arteries in the ocean.

In 1912, the *Titanic* represented science fiction. The world sensed that the twentieth century was going to be explosive with Science and Technology. The *Titanic* was the representation, the reality of an exhilarating understanding that we as a species were beginning at last to travel in amazing ways, either across the ocean or—as with the auto-mobiles—to trundle across paths we even then had begun to smooth across our planet, our Earth.

Chapter Three—The Powerful Lure of Jack and Rose

Part of the hold the *Titanic* exerts on so many of us today is the movie that stars Leonardo DiCaprio and Kate Winslet. This is especially true for women and girls who visit our museum.

When I am assigned to the Grand Staircase, there will usually be one of the young ladies who will pause at the clock at the top of the staircase and pretend to be looking for Jack.

Even young girls are enchanted with the romance of the ship, and for them, for these young girls and older girls and women and even many of the young men, the romance is all about the enchantment of Jack and Rose from the now classic movie that was released in 1997.

Just this past year, there was a girl. I think she was around ten years old, and she was telling all of us at the museum that she was going to grow up and marry Jack.

She was one of the girls who practically swoon when they enter the Grand Staircase at the museum. I am standing there on the second step, dressed as Col. Gracie, smiling and welcoming. But I am not exaggerating when I say that for many of our guests, suddenly being surrounded by the splendor of the Grand Staircase is breathtaking.

We used the original blueprints to recreate the A-deck level of the Grand. There were six decks of the Grand Staircase. The A-deck has something the decks below this one lack—the skylight. Since the A-deck is near the top of the ship, it has the view of this magnificent skylight. Decorated with Edwardian Period designs, it puts us in mind of all the elegance and magnificence *White Star Line* was providing for First Class passengers.

When I am presenting on the Grand Staircase, I get to see such special evidence of how the *Titanic* enchants our guests today and draws them to *Titanic Museum Attraction*. The spectacle of the young ladies insisting that their awkward young men ascend the Grand properly always delights me. The Grand Staircase is the highlight for them, and their young men are going to participate properly whether they want to or not.

It is such fun to watch them. The girl will take her escort's arm and guide him to the proper position for elegantly ascending the Grand. If he resists, she just stops and gives him a look, usually smiling but this is serious, and inevitably the guys sigh and give in, looking embarrassed but knowing it is futile to resist. They proceed to walk up the Grand in a slow, elegant manner, the girls in that moment fully convinced they are wearing beautiful gowns and being escorted by handsome men in tuxedos.

Often, it is the children who first notice the magnificent skylight overarching this deck of the Grand Staircase. A family walks in, usually parents with two or three children. I am welcoming them, letting them know that this is the A-deck of the Grand, built from the original blueprints.

Often one of the youngest of the children will tug at his mother's sleeve and point up toward the skylight.

"Ah, I see that this young person has already noticed a part of the Grand Staircase that delighted First Class passengers."

And we talk about how the skylight was one of many innovations from the *White Star Line.*

“Ships prior to the *Titanic* did have skylights,” I say. “However, they were often stained glass. That made for a darker light. *White Star Line* (the company that managed *Titanic*) wanted a clean, clear light, and finally settled on milk glass.”

Light from outside filters through the milk glass, filling the room with a clear, beautiful light. And if the day is cloudy, the natural light from outside can be supplemented by electric light. The Grand Staircase featured fifty crystal chandeliers scattered throughout the six decks. At night, as well, the electrically lit crystal chandeliers bathed the Grand Staircase decks with a brilliant, clear ambiance.

“We take electricity for granted today,” I mention to our guests. “In 1912, though, electricity was not universally available. Even First Class passengers did not take it for granted.”

There is a quote in the First Class sitting room, the first gallery guests see after ascending the Grand Staircase. An author remarks on the experience of lying down in a luxuriant bed and, with the flick of a single finger, extinguishing the light.

For many Third Class passengers, *Titanic* was the first time they had ever seen electric lights. The ship was a marvel of technology for its day. So much of the excitement of *Titanic* for people of 1912 was due to what was for them cutting-edge technology. The ship itself had the adventure and promise of science fiction. It suggested the adventure, allure, and promise of the future.

But it seems that so much of the powerful hold *Titanic* has for our guests today is sparked by the romance between Jack and Rose in the 1997 classic starring DiCaprio and Winslet. Among all the deep human emotions the *Titanic* stirs in us, this strong, instinctive urge for love and romance between two people captivates and draws us.

Chapter Four—Pieces of History—Titanic Artifacts

Often, I encounter guests as they are descending the Grand Staircase following their tour. They are impressed with how well the museum is presented, and with the many artifacts. We always try to emphasize that these are *authentic* artifacts, not copies, not stage props.

"Whatever you see in a glass case," I say, "has been through a rigorous process of verification. Each one is authentic."

In fact, *Titanic Museum Attraction* in Pigeon Forge is the largest museum of *Titanic* artifacts in the world. The reason we can have such a large, diverse collection of artifacts is that we work with some of the best known private collectors of *Titanic* artifacts in the world.

Collectors often obtain artifacts from Henry Aldridge and Son, a highly prestigious auction company in England. Aldridge and Son is known for taking great pains to authenticate *Titanic* artifacts, a process that involves *Titanic* specialists, scholars, and even laboratories.

One example is the Wallace Hartley violin, auctioned by Aldridge and Son in 2013. The careful process of authentication took some six years and involved numerous *Titanic* specialists and even involved laboratory analysis of a metal plate on the front of the violin.

Guests often ask me how we acquire the hundreds of authentic artifacts on display in our museum. Did we dive to where the *Titanic* rests on the ocean floor today, some two-and-a quarter miles beneath the surface? The answer is that none of the artifacts on display in our museum came from the wreck beneath the surface.

Some of our artifacts were among the items recovered within a week of the sinking. The steamer trunk on display in the first gallery is an example. *Titanic* broke in two before sinking, and there were thousands of items that fell off the ship as it was sinking. Those that could float were bobbing on the surface, creating a debris field stretching for miles. Recovery ships were dispatched to clean up.

Many of our guests wonder about the authentic *White Star Line* china that is on display in our second gallery, the Drawing Room. It was among the items floating after the sinking.

It's true that china does not float. However, what if there are pieces of china hidden within a few of the trunks that were found floating? That is the key to our authentic china. It seems that certain First Class ladies could not resist taking a few souvenirs. The china on display in our Drawing Room was found wrapped in towels in one of the trunks pulled from the debris field.

It may have been understood that a First Class passenger might take something. Last year one of our guests told me he was not at all surprised that First Class ladies on the Titanic might take a few pieces of china.

"One of our family heirlooms," he told me, "is a silver spoon my great grandmother took from the *Andrea Doria* before she sank. My great grandmother always said she had permission to take a souvenir, as long as she didn't abuse the privilege."

After all, the cost of a First Class room on the great liners was high. The *Titanic* was no exception. An average First Class stateroom on the *Titanic* would cost about four hundred thirty dollars. That would be the equivalent of sixteen thousand dollars today.

Our *White Star Line* china represents two of the possibilities for how *Titanic* artifacts survived the sinking: found floating in the debris field is one. Carried off the ship by a passenger is another.

In some cases, when we speak of carrying something off the ship, we are referring to passengers who did not survive. Only three-hundred six bodies were recovered after the sinking. Some items that are valuable *Titanic* artifacts today were found on recovered bodies and sent to family members, if identification was possible.

That is how Edmond Stone's key was preserved. Mr. Stone was a bedroom steward responsible for a number of First Class staterooms on E-Deck. His is a rare master key that would unlock any of the rooms he was responsible for. The key was found in the pocket of his jacket, sent to his family. Today, that key is on display upstairs in the Children's Gallery.

The rare Third Class menu on display was found in the pocket of one of the passengers whose body was recovered. It is badly water stained. It is just possible, though, to read portions of the menu.

In much better shape is a First Class menu on display near the Boiler Room. It was carried off the ship by a passenger who actually survived.

Authentic letters mailed from the *Titanic* represent another kind of artifact. On display in the Shipyard is the original of a letter written by Leonard Taylor, a young crew member. He was writing home to his parents, describing some of his experience on the great ship.

Whenever you see one of these letters, notes, postcards, you are seeing the original.

And finally, there is a group of authentic items from the era. These have been added for context. We want our guests to feel as though they could be part of nineteen twelve, the year *Titanic* sailed. Authentic fliers, advertisements, hand soaps, *White Star Line* menus help our guests feel fully engaged with the world passengers, crew, and the public experienced as they went about the process of living in the first decade of the Twentieth Century. These authentic artifacts are powerful reminders—a connection with the passengers, the crew, and the *Titanic.*

Chapter Five—Breathtakingly Large, Technologically the Future

Titanic Museum Attraction guests and I often reach out together through imagination. For a few moments we linger at the port in Southampton, England, pretending that we are *Titanic's* first passengers waiting for the great ship to appear.

There is a ripple in the crowd as the first among us catches a glimpse of the *Titanic* steaming toward us with a calm, magnificent pace, growing ever larger as it approaches.

"Imagine," I say to our guests, "how overwhelming it is for citizens of 1912 to catch their first glimpse of a vessel that dwarfs previous ships. *Titanic* is nearly twice the size, and she has a new, futuristic design."

"We would have to imagine our reaction today to something that suddenly appears on the Parkway outside our museum. Something beyond our experience."

"It seems to have sailed right off the page of a sketch completed by an artist who imagines some new technology of the future. For people of 1912, however, it is not a sketch. It is the actual, physical representation of that breathtaking new idea of what the future will hold."

Another exciting technology that causes *Titanic* passengers to feel instantly swept into the future is electricity.

Today, we seldom think about how the abundance of electricity onboard *Titanic* creates such a dizzying effect.

It is worth noting that today's technology has come so far that we have become numb to technologies that—though they thrilled the world a hundred years ago—are commonplace today.

Electricity was not universally available in 1912. There were even parts of America that did not have electricity until later in the twentieth century. For many of *Titanic*'s passengers—including the Irish and the Eastern Europeans—*Titanic* might have been their first experience of electric lights.

Think of that!

The *Titanic* has four massive dynamos producing more electricity than many power plants of the early twentieth century. There are ten thousand lights, and they emit a cleaner, brighter light than most people are accustomed to in 1912.

No wonder passengers instantly feel as though they have been swept decades ahead into the future!

Even passengers in First Class and Second Class do not take electric lights for granted.

No doubt, *White Star Line* is aware of how light can dramatically affect how we perceive our world.

"Can you imagine," I ask our guests, "the sheer wonder of entering the A-Deck of the Grand Staircase? Certainly, there is impressive elegance. Shimmering crystal chandeliers, for example, and the burnished, hand-carved woods of the balustrades. Twenty-four-karat, gold-covered medallions catch the eye, and much more."

"But a fullness of light surpassing anything you've experienced on a ship, much less in your home, is nearly a physical blow to your senses."

And yes, even at night the ship glows everywhere with its thousands of clear lights. Even the Grand Staircase skylight is backlit with electric lights at night or on cloudy days. This is a dramatic accomplishment for 1912. Only the *Titanic*, with its four huge electric dynamos, can assail the senses with such wondrous light.

But it does seem that we humans, in every era, become dull and numb with technologies that—while they thrilled when they were new and unexpected—have become ho-hum today.

We require larger and larger creations before we feel awe. Our guests, for example, sometimes express the opinion that our Grand Staircase is smaller than they expect it to be. We did use the original blueprints, though. Our staircase is precisely the same size. However, today we are accustomed to ever larger creations.

Ships the size of the *Titanic* do not awe us today. Our modern ships dwarf the *Titanic*. Such massive creations, they are like floating islands in the sea—especially modern cargo ships. Today's cargo ships have achieved a size unheard of until now.

Who knows what the future will bring?

It may be, however, that the *Titanic* ultimately inspires us less for its technology than for our universal longing in every era to reach toward this *something* we sense just beyond our outstretched fingers.

Today, more than a hundred years after *Titanic* inspired the world, we sense—as humans always have—this vast ocean of Time. It is as though we are riding the swells of the ocean just as the *Titanic* did in April of 1912, always stretching, reaching.

Perhaps the most significant territory that remains to be discovered in our future involves ideas of who we are as humans and what we are becoming, and of why in every era we create our great ships, our wondrous new technologies, always reaching ahead toward new adventures, new wonders, unexplored frontiers.

Chapter Six—Newlyweds Then and Now

The other day I paused to chat with a young couple at the First Class sitting room. The young lady was completely enfolded in the arms of her young man. He whispered something in her ear as I walked in, and she laughed softly, bringing a hand to her mouth. I saw a small but delicately beautiful diamond ring.

I was portraying Father Browne that day, and I gave them what I hoped was a paternal smile as I approached.

"I see you are admiring our First Class sitting room," I said. "You appear to be one of our honeymoon couples."

They both began to nod, a rosy blush creeping up the girl's neck. I could tell they were going to be fun.

"There were twelve honeymoon couples aboard *Titanic,*" I said. "The room you are viewing here is one room of a millionaire suite. This is the sitting room. All the comforts of home. Isn't it beautiful?"

We admired the twenty-four-karat gold leaf trim, which is featured in all First Class areas. There is an electric fireplace, a writing desk, chairs, a sofa, all very inviting.

"Often, I have to resist the temptation of coming into this room and relaxing. It just beckons a person to ease back in one of these comfortable chairs, read, write letters."

And we chatted on about how they really were on their honeymoon. They were from Alabama and had just been married two days ago at their church with family and friends.

"I'm still trying to get all the shaving cream off my car," the young man was telling me. "Or maybe it was whipped cream."

We had fun talking. Other guests had come in and were quietly listening, smiling. I turned to them all and invited them to congratulate our newlyweds, whose names were Michael and Carla. It is often such a warm feeling among guests, as though we become connected somehow through this experience of appreciating the human element that connects us. We identify with those who were on the ship, and, in this case, there was such good will toward our honeymooners.

A gentleman asked, "How much was a First Class room?"

"I'm told," I said, "you would pay four-hundred and thirty dollars for a one-way ticket. Of course, that was 1912 dollars. It would be the equivalent of sixteen thousand dollars today."

First Class, I told them, was expensive, but our First Class passengers were among the wealthiest in the world at that time. Most of them could easily afford the cost.

"As I was saying, though, our First Class sitting room is one of what would have been a three-room suite. In addition to the sitting room, you would have a bedroom, a dining room, and a private promenade deck. In today's money, it would be the equivalent of one hundred twenty-five thousand dollars for a one-way trip."

But then I decided to make this delightful group of guests a special offer.

"In honor of our honeymoon couple," I said, "and because all of you are so interested, I am going to let you be the first to know the news we've just learned."

And I told them that there were only two millionaire suites on the *Titanic*, but this one had just come available.

"J.P. Morgan, whose company provided most of the financial backing for *Titanic*, booked this suite. Unfortunately, business obligations prevented Mr. Morgan from boarding the ship."

I made a little bow, sweeping my arms in an expansive gesture.

"I am delighted to let you be the first to know the room has just come available."

I looked to the men, especially, as I related more good news.

"You gentlemen appear to be distinguished and among those to whom we would make this unprecedented offer. And because we are on day two of the voyage, I believe I can arrange with the purser to upgrade you today for only one hundred thousand dollars."

The guests are smiling by this time and shaking their heads.

"I'm sure your vouchers, checks, cards will be honored here."

Of course, we are all just having fun, but we're learning actual information about the ship. There really were two millionaire suites of the description I gave. J.P. Morgan had booked one of the two. An interesting entrepreneur—Lady Charlotte Cardeza—booked the second of the two millionaire suites, and she was onboard.

Bruce Ismay took the second of the millionaire suites when J.P. Morgan was unable to make the trip. It was Bruce Ismay, director of the *White Star Line,* and Lord Pirrie, head of Harland and Wolff shipyard, who sketched out rough plans for the *Titanic* on napkins after dinner one night.

And as for our honeymoon couple? One of the gentlemen had become fully engaged in the experience of being whisked off to another time, and the opportunity to be the richest man on the ship.

This guest stepped forward and said, "I would like to speak to the purser about upgrading this honeymoon couple to the millionaire suite."

He handed me his boarding pass with a flourish, as though presenting his calling card. I stepped back in amazement.

"Yes, Mr. Astor," I said, smiling at the other guests. And then, to the honeymoon couple, I said, "Mr. Astor here would like to add his good wishes by upgrading your room to a millionaire suite. How fortunate." I turned to the other guests. "Perhaps we should all add our congratulations and best wishes."

We began to applaud the newlyweds.

By then, another group of guests was entering, smiling and probably wondering why we are applauding the blushing couple. The girl was wiping her eyes with a tissue.

I held out my arms to the guests just entering, inviting them in.

"Please join us in congratulating our honeymooners, Michael and Carla, and in acknowledging John Jacob Astor here, who has graciously offered to upgrade their room to one of our two millionaire suites!"

We were all smiling, applauding, and I knew we had created an experience for our newlyweds that they would never forget. All of us enjoyed being a part of sharing in their joy as we became passengers onboard this great ship, *Titanic.*

And this is an example of what we attempt to do every day at *Titanic Museum Attraction.* For us, it is all about bringing another world, another time to life for our guests, and conveying for a while at this world-class museum the experience of another era.

Chapter Seven—How Children Experience Titanic Museum Attraction

I am overwhelmed by what I sense in the children who visit our museum. First, there is a wild, powerful genetic signature within them. And I understand that this flinging forward of our DNA into each new era connects us with all our species who have ever lived.

There is a strange uneasiness I feel as I stand before these young people—at the Map, for example. We refer to our very first gallery as the Map Room because it features a big map which tracks *Titanic*'s planned voyage. Beginning in Southampton, England, the ship then sails across the English Channel to Cherbourg, France. Overnight, it's on to Queenstown, Ireland, and from there on to New York City.

It is as though I see these children from a distance, their eyes as reflective of the entire, poignant human experience as anything. Something that reverberates, like an endless line of linked pins trailing delicately, gracefully, tracing some elusive, shifting path back toward when our human line began.

The children's eyes are wide, with pigment as fresh and clear as if it has come from the most unadulterated, sublime palate of an artist whose genius far surpasses that of the best the human gene pool has ever produced.

There is also their keen intelligence. When they are deeply into the story I am telling them, it is as though I am riveted in their attention, their keen minds curious and processing.

Children skip over to the Map, some of them wearing clean, fresh outfits of deep, nautical blue with little anchors to reflect their visit to this museum. The children come, and I see the inquisitive depths of their eyes. I am held within the calipers of their curious intelligence, scrutinized thoughtfully as they slip into that trancelike mindset which produces, we are told, certain brainwaves akin to when we are deeply involved in learning.

Perhaps I see them as even their parents may not, because their attention is focused on me as I deliver my presentation, catching them up in the rhythm of story that carries them to the moment, the ship, the reality of a time that is past and yet lives again within this story.

I sense this connection that binds us, and I can nearly see this elusive, dusky, shifting line that somehow represents us. It traces our line through the bends and curves until it arrives at the point where our species was first created.

Recently, I have been reminded of the fear experienced by children. On the night of the *Titanic* sinking, they must have been terrified in the chaos, the violence. There is such a sinister, wild survival instinct unleashed when disaster bursts upon us, and we are facing threats to our existence.

Even now, though, at our museum children may experience fear.

In all my eight years at our museum I have never seen anything quite like the behavior of two four-year old girls who stood before me at the Map. They were precious and beautiful with blonde hair and beautiful eyes of deep, rich pigment.

Of course, this beauty in our children is not unusual. But one of the little girls encircled her arms around the other, and they stood together, quiet and still, as though facing some imminent disaster. All of us noticed, and it was a moving picture. I noticed a ripple spread through the adults as they responded, smiling. The girls looked so precious.

At one point in my presentation I paused and said, "I can tell that these girls must be best friends."

Several in the group smiled and nodded as we marveled at this intriguing display. It moved us and called to something deep within each one of us that we didn't even know was there.

I realized that the little girl who was being hugged was scared, possibly frightened at what she might experience at our museum. Probably she had heard there were scary things associated with *Titanic,* a ship that sank with passengers who were badly frightened. Perhaps she had heard that many did not survive.

So, this one four-year-old was comforting the other, embracing her and offering her own strength, as though she understood and was compassionate and offering protection.

So many moving impulses emanate from primal, instinctive depths within us. No doubt many of these were evident in the *Titanic* disaster. And yet what I observe among our museum guests—particularly among families with children—demonstrates that we are much the same now. We have deeply riven, powerful surges within us. The best within us is beautiful. There are many moments at *Titanic Museum Attraction* when I am privileged to observe these.

Many are connected with fear. The other night, for example, I encountered a father with two young children. I was portraying Father Browne at the Grand Staircase that night. The little boy was sobbing, wailing, and his father was trying to reassure him that there was nothing to be afraid of. I stepped from the staircase and nodded at the father before leaning down to reassure the boy, another four-year old.

“It’s okay,” I said softly. "This is a nice museum.”

I was a little surprised when the boy backed away from me, seeming even more upset.

“No,” he kept repeating, staring at me. “I don’t want pirates.”

I glanced at his little sister, who seemed okay, and then at the father. I was confused, but then in a flash realized what it was.

“Oh, my goodness,” I chuckled. “He’s afraid of *me*.”

Sometimes we don’t realize how we must look through the eyes of young children. As Father Browne, I was wearing a long black robe and a strange black hat—a priest’s attire. But to this little boy, I was a pirate, perhaps Blackbeard himself, or someone similar.

Certainly, children on the *Titanic*’s lifeboats needed comforting. First Class passenger Edith Rosenbaum recounted how children in her lifeboat were whimpering and crying. She decided to distract them by turning the tail of her toy pig, which caused a music box inside the pig to play a happy tune. Most of the children were fascinated and stopped crying.

The other night, at our museum, I did the only thing I could think of to help the father soothe his frightened little boy. I explained the father’s predicament to our

Manager on Duty, Cole, who said, "no problem", and arranged for them to return on a future date to continue their tour through our *Titanic Museum Attraction,* where so much of what speaks to us involves connections between humans then and now.

Chapter Eight—Penguins, Sharks, and Treasure

Dressed as First Class passenger Col. Archibald Gracie, I awaited the frisky group at the Map, which is the first gallery in our world-class museum. And yes, frisky is the word. There were two children skipping, pirouetting, humming what sounded like the theme from Walt Disney's *Frozen*.

There was a dark-haired little girl of maybe five years trotting beside her younger brother, whose name she later confided in me was Cody, though I never did learn the girl's name.

But yes, I suspected this would be one of those delightful groups when the dark-haired little girl suddenly stopped and flung her arms wide as though embracing a wondrous something too amazing at first to even identity. But then, she did identify it exuberantly.

"Oh, Mommy, look," she exclaimed, "Oh, it's a treasure chest!"

Brother Cody approached it cautiously, with the reluctance of a born skeptic. He looked almost scientific as he eyed it, not yet willing to concede. I could see it in his face. His sister might be a year or so older, but he watched her with the understanding that she was prone to absurd pronouncements and perhaps needed his steady consideration of the thing before confirming that an actual treasure chest could have been on the *Titanic*.

"Yes," I said, smiling at the girl and her little brother. "It does look like a treasure chest, doesn't it?"

I explained that it is like a big suitcase that people of more than a hundred years ago used when they took a voyage across the ocean. Known as a steamer trunk, it was definitely onboard the *Titanic*. It belonged to a Third Class passenger. The *Titanic* broke in two before sinking, and this trunk was one of thousands of items that fell out of the ship as it was sinking.

"Those items that could float were bobbing around on the surface. Recovery ships were immediately dispatched to clean up what was then considered a dangerous mess. The debris field went on for miles."

Cody stood before me with a stern expression, his eyes fixed upon me. Meanwhile, his dark-haired sister discovered something to fiddle with on her sneaker. I began to tell of *Titanic*'s voyage, which started in Southampton, England.

"April tenth, 1912," I said. "One of those days when you can just feel the excitement. It was a celebration, the first day of the first voyage of the great *Titanic*."

That's when the dark-haired little girl popped up, bumping against brother Cody, who let out an offended moan, turning to his parents, his facial expression suggesting–without words–the idea, *Did you see what she just did?* His sister, unperturbed, stood on tiptoe, raising her hands as she exclaimed, "I just love penguins!"

Others had come over to join the group by now, smiling and nodding at the dark-haired girl's excited proclamation. The parents looked at me apologetically, leaning forward to whisper for the girl to just listen.

But that was my cue to grab this sudden reference to penguins and weave it into the presentation. After all, hadn't Col. Archibald Gracie, the passenger I was pretending to be, resembled a penguin out there on that night, balancing atop a capsized lifeboat?

"How interesting that you would mention penguins," I said. "That reminds me how I had to stand on capsized Collapsible Lifeboat B with my arms out like this . . ."

I held my arms out to either side.

". . . on the capsized lifeboat where I and thirty other men stood like penguins as we tried to balance on top of that overturned lifeboat as the *Titanic* was sinking."

And I nodded to the guests who had just joined the group.

"Col. Archibald Gracie," I informed them, "was washed off the sinking *Titanic* by a wave, was able to reach a capsized lifeboat known as Collapsible Lifeboat B, and stood like this—arms out to side—balancing for hours with thirty other men until the *Carpathia* arrived."

The *Carpathia* was the first ship to arrive in response to the distress call. It arrived around 4 a.m., an hour and forty minutes after the *Titanic* sank.

I then returned to the Map, tracing the route from Southampton, to Cherbourg, to Queenstown, and from there to where the lookouts called down to the Navigating Bridge, "Iceberg Right Ahead!"

That was when the dark-haired little girl, who seemed lost in thought about penguins, looked up expectantly.

"Sharks?" she cried, her voice rising. "There were sharks?"

Apparently when I said *Iceberg right ahead* she heard not *Iceberg* but *Shark*. Such an exuberant child, such imagination. I noticed that brother Cody had adopted a look of resignation. He caught my eye with an expression as if to convey the idea of his long suffering in the face of her outbursts. It was as though he were saying, *She's always like this.*

"Oh," I said. "Yes, maybe sharks. Just maybe, but we really don't know for sure."

I was not surprised to see that the group at the Map seemed to be thoroughly enjoying the dark-haired little girl, and now they were smiling at her little brother, who had begun to nibble the lower right-hand corner of his boarding pass.

These children, though. Each one is such an effervescing package of promise, creativity, and potential. They and their families are living proof that we have so much in common with *Titanic* passengers, which included one hundred thirty-three children and their families—the same surge of new life and the ever-present hope and plans that define us now just as they did more than a hundred years ago.

In truth, this ever-present surge is always with us, reminding us of the effervescing rhythms of the sea, of the constant movement of surf as it bubbles and stretches up a flat beach. Just as it always has in every era of human history, and long before humans were here.

We are part of this eternal cycle. The *Titanic* allows us to look from the perspective of a hundred years or so ahead of *Titanic*'s era, feeling this ever- present tug as we consider just how closely *Titanic* passengers resemble who we are now, in our own time. As a matter of fact, we today, and *Titanic* passengers in 1912, resemble all humans who have ever struggled toward life upon this planet, Earth, where our species was first begun.

Chapter Nine—A Ten-Year Old Autistic Boy's Titanic Dream

I was assigned to our Discovery Gallery for a few hours yesterday and thoroughly enjoyed interacting with our guests about the 26-foot-long, 56-thousand-piece Lego ship. Built by Brynjar Karl, an autistic ten-year old from Iceland, the ship is an inspiring tribute to human achievement.

I was surprised with how open our young guests were in their admiration of the accomplishment. Two boys were visiting from Houston, and they told me they were getting ideas for their own projects. They have built a much smaller *Titanic* and plan to make a film featuring it.

"But this . . ." said the older of the two, gesturing with his hands toward Brynjar Karl's magnificent *Titanic*."

He trailed off, just shaking his head in wonder.

His brother made me laugh when he said, "And I thought my Lego Death Star was something."

I had fascinating conversations with many of the adults, as well. One man shared his own experience with his autistic granddaughter. He told me of how she loves to read and has stacks of her favorite books.

"Sometimes at bedtime I'm reading to her, and I think she's already asleep, and I'll skip ahead. The other night she opened one eye, took the book from my hand and turned back to the place where I had been reading before skipping."

After we chatted a bit more about how special these autistic children are, he looked thoughtful and said, "You know, maybe we're the ones with challenges."

In other words, we who assume we're the normal ones are perhaps comparatively less in many ways.

Certainly, autism often comes with enhanced abilities.

I very much enjoyed my several hours sharing Brynjar Karl's *Titanic* with our guests. Such proofs of what is possible call to something deep within each of us. The Lego *Titanic* is a fitting conclusion to a tour of *Titanic Museum Attraction*, which showcases a major accomplishment for society in the early years of the Twentieth Century, more than a century ago.

Our entire museum Crew were moved when Brynjar, his mother and his grandfather visited the museum in the Spring of 2018. It would be our dramatic presentation of Brynjar's *Titanic*, now on display in the Discovery Gallery.

What a day that was. All the Crew, dressed in our best, lined both sides of the Grand Staircase as the tall, imposing Lowell Lytle, who is our Captain Smith, welcomed Brynjar and then escorted him, his mom, and grandfather on a tour of the museum.

The entire Crew then moved to the Discovery Gallery, preparing to meet Brynjar and his family with a formal greeting, the officers saluting crisply and the maids curtsying as they entered.

And then it was time for them to see the stunning video which plays on three huge screens as our guests view Brynjar's remarkable ship. We were so touched to see them there, Brynjar, his mom, his grandfather, as they saw his incredible Lego *Titanic* for the first time beautifully displayed at our museum. As the video lit up the screens behind Brynjar's ship, we were moved to see the proud grandfather place a hand affectionately on

Brynjar's shoulder as strong emotions clearly swept over them.

Afterwards, we had many opportunities to interact with Brynjar and his family. Brynjar's mom told of how Brynjar's autism—when he was much younger—meant that he spoke very little and did not communicate easily. However, his *Titanic* project brought such attention and opportunities for interaction with diverse, supportive, adoring fans.

Gradually, he began to talk, eventually developing an ease in communicating so that the average person would never suspect that he had faced challenges such as speaking. In fact, while in Pigeon Forge, Brynjar enthusiastically accepted the offer to speak to hundreds of students at schools in the area, telling his story and answering their many questions.

I found him to be an engaging person, fascinating to interact with. I was somewhat surprised to find that I now have to literally look up to him. Yes, it is true that Brynjar was ten-years old when he built this 56-thousand Lego *Titanic*. However, as of his visit to *Titanic Museum Attraction* in 2018, he is a tall, engaging sixteen-year old. Flip over to the photos included near the end of this book, and you'll see what I mean.

Chapter Ten—The Feminine Response—Ever the Same

A behind-the-scenes area at the *Titanic Museum Attraction* in Pigeon Forge, TN is called Scotland Road. The area includes a galley, a dressing room, and lockers. I was preparing to dress as Father Francis Browne, the Jesuit priest-in-training who captured the only photographs we have of life on board the *Titanic.*

My new socks came packaged with a plastic fastener, and I was looking for something to snip the fastener. I needed nail clippers and was asking some of the girl Crew Members—First Class maids at the museum—if they might help.

Lauren had kept silent, fiddling with something in her lap as she knelt before her locker. I think it may have been Sarah who found a small pair of cuticle scissors in a little zipper pouch in her locker. After I snipped the plastic and put on my socks, I returned to the locker area to find Lauren gravely snipping one of her fingernails with clippers.

"Oh, I see now," I said, teasing her. "Here I was desperate to find fingernail clippers, and there Lauren had some all along."

Lauren looked a little sheepish and kept fiddling with the clippers, fidgeting as she aimed them at a ragged part of her index fingernail.

"Well," she said. "I didn't know what you wanted them for. I imagined you wanted to trim your toenails."

She looked so miserably awkward and defensive, this girl kneeling on the carpet near her locker, manipulating the clippers. I felt one of those moments when it was more than just a routine day preparing to dress as Father Browne and walk through the door—the one with the sign that reads: *You Are Now entering 1912.*

Much of the fascination I feel in my role at *Titanic Museum Attraction* lies in my sense that no matter what the era, we are connected. I feel this when I observe our guests—individuals, children, families—who have the same hopes, needs, and human characteristics, as others who have lived before us.

And on the day of the fingernail clippers, I was aware that Lauren is a girl who resembles any of the females who have ever lived with that signature, feminine awareness of the male in all his unpleasant ways.

It is this primal, inner stuff that sometimes rises within us when we least suspect it. It is a breath rising and is one of the clues to what we have been. As we are here, walking with our graceful human gait so casually in our own time upon the planet, we are the reflection of all of those who preceded us on this strange, enticing world upon which we are caught.

Lauren, in that moment of confession, was a little shy and awkward to admit this deeply seated, uniquely feminine distaste for the toenails of another, and particularly the toenails of a male not her mate. But her reaction reflects some of who we are as humans and who we have been.

There is much that connects us in Time, and the *Titanic* included a number of women who were paving the way for more choices, more equality. We have a tribute to these women in the Memorial Room. It is called *The*

Amazing Women of the Titanic and features their portraits and a brief synopsis of what each one of them did.

Part of history, though, is the rather surprising fact that a hundred years ago, women could not even vote. One of *Titanic's* Amazing Women—Margaret Tobin Brown (a.k.a. the unsinkable Molly Brown) ran for the U.S. Senate before women could vote. An early women's suffragist, Margaret Brown was not to be denied.

Women finally were awarded the right to vote in 1920. It took a Constitutional Amendment to make it official, but of course that was one step of many. Changes slowly began to take effect throughout the twentieth century. Women today occasionally remind me that they're still not quite there yet.

Just this past year, I was giving a tour to a group of young sorority women from a university. We had paused in the Drafting Room and were discussing the overwhelming challenge of creating plans for *Titanic* and her sister ship, the *Olympic.*

A photograph of the beautiful Drafting Room at Harland and Wolff shipyard takes up nearly the entire wall. With its barrel ceiling, inset with skylights to emit the light needed by these draftsmen, the room is quite impressive.

I usually ask the question, "What do we not see in this photograph that we would naturally expect to see today? Consider that this is a huge project and involves talent and skills for precision and the creation of blueprints."

One of the young women raised her hand, a serious look on her face.

"Women," she said. "Those draftsmen are all men. Every single one of them."

The others in her group were nodding now, agreeing with this observation, and I had to agree as well. Though the answer I expected was the absence of computers, these young women were correct. Margaret Tobin Brown would have seconded their observation.

Chapter Eleven—We Sense Ourselves and Our History in the Sea

When I was very young, my father was a salesman for Proctor & Gamble, a soap company based in Cincinnati, and we moved often from one little Kentucky town to another.

Wherever we were, though, we kids sailed blocks of Ivory Soap in the big, claw-footed bath tubs that always seemed to be included in the houses we lived in. We were unflinchingly loyal to Proctor & Gamble products, and we hissed and booed products manufactured by Lever Brothers, the competition.

Ivory Soap wrappers included paper cutouts of sails and tiny sticks which could be masts. Perhaps my fascination with sailing ships began right there in those claw-footed bathtubs, sailing Ivory Soap boats. But the ocean always powerfully called to this presence I had from an early age felt tugging something deep within me.

I remember one of my first trips to the ocean when I stood at the edge of the surf with my sister, Jeanie. I was overcome with a giddy sensation as the frothy, hissing sheets of surf crept up the flat beach to where we stood.

Looking down at the water as it paused and then began its backwards pull, drawn back toward the immensity of the ocean, we were swept into an intense feeling of vertigo. It was as if we would be sucked out with it, and the rush of excitement and the experience of this new sensation was an immense delight.

I was no more than fourteen at the time. I had lived my entire life in the mountains of Appalachia and sensed something powerful in the dip of the mineral air, in the pungent odor of Sugar Maple and Birch, and in the loamy earth. My experience of the sea added another powerful sense of this *something* that has always mesmerized human beings, no matter what the era.

In this experience of the sea and its cascading run along the flat beach, something deep within me stirred. I felt myself beginning to dip a cautious toe into these invisible areas. I was drawn to them and determined to grasp, though sometimes it seemed I grasped only empty air.

I had begun to reach toward something I felt trembling and fragile deep within me. It was something for which there was really no teaching. Perhaps in some cultures there were teachers who could guide a hesitant, shy adolescent toward this area. However, I had no help. Not really.

The *Titanic*, an incredible ship, was associated with the adventure of the sea. There is much that calls something deep within us in every age as the sea powerfully, rhythmically, continues to slide in toward the shore. The sea interacts in its own timeless fashion with the intricate systems which are unchanged since our beginnings here upon this planet.

Perhaps, though, no life on our planet has a concept of time as rigid as humans do. We are pleased to live much longer than the grubs, the centipedes, the fruit flies and the delicate swarms of gnats dipping and rising in the air. We are largely indifferent to the subtleties that surround and call to us.

This may be an idea that certainly includes our own fragile planet but extends to the Universe and beyond. It is a tapestry of intricate, gossamer fibers constructed of the light that effervesces across the vastness—light that is not unlike the sea that has long enticed us here upon Earth.

During a typical day at our *Titanic Museum Attraction*, I have the sense that the essence of what fascinates us and draws us toward the *Titanic* is that it is like a thumbnail sketch of who we are and what we are becoming. In the specifics of the *Titanic* story, we see ourselves.

But yes, I observe these families who visit our museum—parents with their children, these family units which have been the nucleus of each generation in any era. I am awed by the literal flinging forth of new generations and feel a connection with all who have gone before.

As I've mentioned, I have this sense that we are somehow connected with all who have lived before—all the humans from every era, all the way back to our beginnings. And if it is true that we are connected, then we can sense these others. Something within us tugs.

As I glimpse the world of our time, I see evidence of who we are now and what we have been. There are leafy trees and lush grass. There are swimming pools, and the laughter and squeals of delight rising from children splashing in the water are no different from what we might have heard in the world of thousands of years ago.

Water flows down from a toadstool-shaped platform balanced on a pedestal, inviting the children to splash and stomp on the smooth concrete base. In these moments, life effervesces with the delight of a new place and with the ancient human joy of water and sun that has flittered along earth and grass since time out of mind. Surely there are mysteries here that we seldom, if ever, pause to think about.

Crew Members at *Titanic Museum Attraction* are encouraged to become intimately familiar with the *Titanic* and its passengers and crew. We want our guests feel as though they are part of that time and can experience the ship. Sometimes, I feel that I was there myself and am carried away by imaginings.

Yes, the ship is nearly twice the size of earlier ships. It is an incredible accomplishment. But as I am here, as I consider this great ship and what it means, it is as though I am aware of all who have gone before us.

Chapter Twelve—Titanic: A Cross-Section of Evolving Humanity

As I experience the full range of our museum, which for me includes the guests, the people, the human *beings* of our day, I cannot help myself. I return to the idea that we have much in common with all those humans who have lived before us on this fragile planet with its delicate ecosystems, atmosphere, and the oceans that we have barely even begun to explore.

One fact concerning the *Titanic* that we usually do not discuss or think about involves the beginnings of how our species has damaged the oceans. It appears that all the waste products, the sewage, was simply discharged from the *Titanic*—and other ships—into the sea. Today, most of us would cringe at the thought. I hope that we are becoming more aware. And yet, sadly, one part of what we have in common with humans of the *Titanic's* era is this pesky tendency to pollute.

No, ships today do not discharge sewage into the oceans. Or at least they're not supposed to. However, we are polluting the oceans in all sorts of ways. If I were to put a finger on what it is that defines us in every age, it would include this tendency not to care about how we are damaging the fragile ecosystems of our planet.

Or, perhaps we do care on one level. But then our eagerness to have what we feel we need surpasses whatever caring we have. Isn't it interesting that our drive to reach beyond ourselves, to explore and to achieve new knowledge, technologies, and abilities often damages our planet? We are like eager, precocious, and reckless children in our impatient, self-centered rush toward the exhilarating new frontiers that we discover in every era.

And of course, the *Titanic* is a symbol for that stretch, that rush forward. There it is, magnificent, a thing of breathtaking beauty, a new design that suggests the future and new, thrilling technology for its day.

Another part of this sense of the stretch forward includes the movers and shakers who were part of *Titanic*'s maiden voyage. Many of these wealthy men would gather in the First Class smoking room, snipping off the ends of fat cigars before lighting and puffing them.

But that is another of the human markers that define us. In every age, our attitudes and assumptions are shifting. Wc hopc wc are growing more mature, more perceptive, less conceited and selfish. Whatever strides we make come with great battles, upheavals. Perhaps they are growing pains.

The *Titanic* was, indeed, the floating palace Bruce Ismay and Lord Pirrie initially set out to build. But it was also a floating cross-section of evolving humanity. In this collection of humans from the poorest to the wealthiest, we see ourselves. *Titanic* is a snapshot of who we were then, which is not so different from who we are now: all our wrinkles, blemishes, and warts, as well as the best of what we are striving to become. And that is a large part of why the *Titanic* continues to fascinate us today.

Another reason, though, for our fascination may be that the *Titanic* disaster reminds us of our own vulnerability. It sketches in stark detail images of people like all of us. Part of the predicament of being human is our frailty, our inevitable confrontation with finality.

And the *Titanic* disaster is in a sense a grim painting of what we must all eventually come to terms with. Here they were, all these individuals, trusting in the promise that they were fortunate to be here on the cutting edge of the best. Indeed, *Titanic* was the very representation of the adventure of new technology.

And safe? Yes, it was accepted by most everyone that *Titanic* was the safest ship ever constructed. *Titanic* and her sister ship the *Olympic*. Truly, these modeled the future. They *were* the thrilling reality of what the twentieth century would offer. Even beyond the twentieth, society was literally singing and dancing to the latest hits as they toasted the epitome of ships. The entire voyage was to be a magnificent proof of her promise.

And perhaps we today get a little jolt of gruesome identification with their plight. There they are, so much like us, with our plans and celebrations. Our hopes and the tender relationships with family, the determined march ahead toward what we hope will bring security, pleasure, entertainment.

Then, with an electrifying suddenness, it is all jerked away. It is nearly as though a curtain has been torn aside. All the softness and warmth upon the ship, the abundance of light, the scent of tantalizing dinners steaming in the galleys, the kaleidoscope of visuals and promise of absolute safety on the epitome of this incredible vessel. It is a ship so far ahead of its time. *Titanic* is science fiction for its era.

And it is stripped from them with such suddenness. Perhaps that is what we identify with most. We all have unconscious fears of when such a time will inevitably come for us. We feel a genuine connection with these living individuals. The spectacle of their sudden thrust from the luxurious environment of a magnificent ship into the starkness of a freezing night. There they are, with the awful reality of that night, the immense universe glittering above them. Beautiful, and yet on this night seeming so indifferent to their situation.

Their ship of dreams is sinking. The *unsinkable Titanic* is shifting beneath their feet, the decks steeper and steeper. And so many trapped, unable to get a lifeboat. It is a horrific event we examine with grim fascination, relieved that we are not part of that nightmare even as we shudder. Like them, we are vulnerable humans, subject to some eventual confrontation with an end.

Titanic fascinates for many reasons. Surely it is a symbol of how the human species is always reaching with enthusiasm toward the adventure of new technology. And the spectacle of its fate causes us to swallow hard, fascinated and yet sobered by what it was like for individuals so suddenly thrust from comfort and security into a freezing, harsh encounter with death.

Chapter Thirteen—Something Out There Just Beyond Our Grasp

On April 14, 1912, a Sunday morning, many of the *Titanic* passengers gathered in groups in various parts of the ship to sing hymns and to reflect upon how we all need a spiritual lifeboat, as Fr. Thomas Byles pointed out in his sermon. Of course, neither he nor any of the crew, and not even Captain Edward John Smith himself, suspected for a moment that this great ship, said to be unsinkable, would ever run afoul of anything that could sink her, be it iceberg, reef, squall, or anything the wondrous ship might encounter upon the tumultuous sea.

No, for them the *Titanic* was a monument to our human drive to always push toward new frontiers as we linger here, always preparing to leap ahead with the delicate spring of a deer or the pounce of a lion. It is the one thing that defines us, this craving for adventure, the mesmerizing unknown which entices just beyond our outstretched fingertips.

Today, the *Titanic* is a monument to this craving. It is, I believe, a good metaphor for who we are and what we are striving to become. In every generation, there is our drive to leap yet a bit further into the mesmerizing possibilities, the lure of our future.

I remember the man just last week who stood before an authentic deck chair from the *Titanic.* I walked over to him and said, "Yes, this deck chair was found floating after the sinking. It is one of only seven surviving deck chairs from the *Titanic.*"

He looked at me for a long moment. "You're telling me that this chair was actually onboard that ship? It is not a replica?"

I assured him that it is authentic, and that any artifact that is displayed in a glass case at our museum is authentic. The man was quiet for a full ten or fifteen seconds. As I turned to walk away, he slowly shook his head.

"If these artifacts could only talk," he said.

And his words, uttered in a soft, furry whisper, nudged that similar, related curiosity within me. How many times have I myself stood before one of these artifacts and felt something go bump in the depths of me, like the wooden hull of a bunged-up rowboat?

There is a sort of rowboat within me, you know. Or I would say it is the image of such a boat, old with dark green paint that is peeling to reveal sun-bleached wood. It is the persistent nudge we feel when confronted by relics such as these artifacts. They jostle something deep within us.

The *Titanic* began her maiden voyage on April 10, 1912. The culture that built this ship was a world different from our own in many respects. However, I believe that one reason the *Titanic* nudges that something deep inside us is that on some level we understand that there are fundamental similarities that define humans in any era.

The society of *Titanic*'s day felt this same, all-consuming yearning for what is out there just beyond our outstretched fingers. I nearly used the term *might be* out there just beyond us. But it isn't a matter of *might be*, is it? Each of us, when we are deeply honest, sense this with an intuitive understanding. There is something within each of us, and this something seems to be a largely unexplored facet of the human experience. It is one of the markers that define us, yet we scarcely give it much thought.

The *Titanic* draws upon this elusive something that is there, swinging with the mesmerizing, slow rhythm of one of the bunged-up, sun-bleached rowboats tied to an ancient dock with a piece of gnarled, weathered rope.

Just as that man who pondered the deck chair, we gaze at these relics tossed overboard even as *Titanic* was sinking. They were floating on the surface in the immediate aftermath of the tragedy. A debris field stretched for miles. Recovery ships were dispatched, and thousands of items were collected during the next several weeks.

That deck chair is one of the many items found floating upon the surface of the sea, grim tokens of the breakup of a brilliant symbol of our human reach toward this something that each of us feels, restlessly swaying upon currents deep within us. They are knocking with the rhythm of a weathered wooden rowboat bumping against the supports of some forgotten dock. They are waiting for us to explore elusive regions deep within us with the enthusiasm we have until now reserved only for what we can touch and see and build.

Surely the *Titanic* was a monument to this inner need, this human quest to always reach for this something we sense. *Something* out there, just beyond our grasp.

Chapter Fourteen—The Titanic Band Plays On Until the Bitter End

In our culture, we extol the young. Their physical forms exhibit the glory of this genetic clock unwinding within us with a steady, unforgiving beat. As steady and sure as the precise flicker of a metronome, one of those clocklike counters set high on a shelf, hovering near a piano, perhaps, measuring the beat.

It is something we have designed to help keep time, a help to one of the venerable, wizened music teachers, one leg casually crossed over another, his palm tapping out the beat, a distant smile on his face as though the music his pupil struggles to capture has taken him back to some part of his own youth. Years ago, he was the spry, lithesome lad courting this incredible dark-eyed girl with fabulous, curving lines, and he remembers the delicate slope of her jaw as she tosses her head and laughs.

In every era, in every human culture, there is music, and it was splendidly in evidence on the maiden voyage of the *Titanic*. There were eight musicians: the *Titanic* band, whose music created much of the atmosphere in First Class.

Isn't it true that music has such a powerful effect on us?

Do we pause to think about why it is there, this music that surrounds us? So much is there that we do not pause to think about, but music is nearly always somewhere near for most of us. It draws something from deep within. We are creatures who respond, sometimes calmed, at other times we are lifted on crescendos of such amazing rhythms that we can scarcely do anything other than dance.

So yes, of course, it was an important part of the *Titanic* experience. If you were a First Class passenger, you would be given a little music book, very thin, just a few pages. We have one of these on display in the museum. The booklet appears to be little more than front-and-back covers with perhaps a few pages between. This thin booklet only contains a few pages, a listing of more than three hundred song titles.

First Class passengers were encouraged to call out a title, and the musicians would immediately play the requested song. Whatever it was, classical or jazz or popular songs of the day.

But yes, I do believe these reverberations jostle something deep within us, something primal, instinctive, an unconscious need and a mostly forgotten understanding of who we are. The music reverberates, a barely perceptible movement of the air in the chill of evening as familiar stars revolve and spangle the sky above our planet.

As a Crew Member of *Titanic Museum Attraction,* I have so often coaxed guests into that night, as though we are there as *Titanic* scrapes along the iceberg, and the musicians move out onto the boat deck. They even trundle out one of the Steinway pianos, and then play, merging the soft cries of their instruments into what ended with plaintive notes of hymns. Tradition says that the last song played was one of bandleader Wallace Hartley's favorites: *Nearer My God to Thee.*

It is so cold, and there comes the shocking, shrieking scream of all the steam being vented simultaneously from the boilers. They must release the pent-up steam from the boilers, for the ship has stopped.

After the tumultuous, thunderous escape of all that pent-up pressure, there is silence surrounding *Titanic,* said to be the safest ship ever built. *Titanic* is the hope of its era, and there are high expectations for the future.

Suddenly, *Titanic* is dead in the water, and an eerie quiet descends. Voices of officers sound flat and dead in the cold air. Lifeboats bump as they swing in their davits. There are the shouts of frustrated crewmen attempting to swing lifeboats out and down.

The musicians stand in their black working suits, their highly trained fingers plucking strings or maneuvering violin bows, or pressing the ivory keys of a new Steinway. Music lifts spirits for a while, attempting to defy the reality of this outrage. It is the ridiculous predicament of a ship invested with the hopes and the pride of its time, dead in the water. *Titanic* is becoming leaden as the weight of all that water spills into her lower levels.

And still, the musicians stoically play. There is, come to think of it, a saying that came from this incident: *And the band played on.* And it is true. The band played until the bitter end, twenty-eight-degree saltwater eventually rising to soak their shoes, invade their socks, cramp the muscles in their feet. And at first, yes, the music seems to create a sense that perhaps it isn't so bad, especially for the hour or so when most could believe that the ship was not sinking.

Surely, *Titanic* could never sink. After all, isn't it said to be unsinkable? Isn't it the magical, incandescent bauble launched by a society just easing into the twentieth century with the elegance and grace of brilliant new design and potential?

It is said they shift to hymns during the last thirty minutes before the ship sinks. Tradition has it that the very last song played is *Nearer My God to Thee.* There is a quote in our Music Gallery from Second Class passenger Charlotte Collyer, who said she was quite certain that was the last song.

Think of it, though. If you are left on the ship with no recourse. None, because the lifeboats have all been launched. And it is surreal, unbelievable that just a short while earlier you had been part of a ship of light and warmth, glamour and elegant strains of music and—for First Class passengers—elaborate eleven-course dinners in the evenings. You were among some of the most famous people in the world on a ship that was the future. Snug, secure, and feeling invincible, as the ship was said to be.

And then, in no more than a few moments, you are out there in the cold, the reality of the magnificent heavens above you, the sharp, clear stars, and the grim realization that all is stripped away, and you are minutes from death. And that, ladies and gentlemen, is what fascinates and tugs at this deep *something* within us. It is our predicament as humans, that we are here for a short while and then must face death. It may come soon, it may come later.

We are all like the passengers and crew of the RMS *Titanic.* The story resonates with us. It resonates deeply, indeed.

And yes, the band plays on. Until the bitter end, music wafts across the sea, reaching those in the lifeboats who watch in shock and deep dismay as the great *Titanic* goes down before their eyes, the distant strains of the band playing that last hymn, *Nearer My God to Thee.*

Chapter Fifteen—We Are Connected in Every Era Through Our Children

I must return to the children who add much to the experience of the museum. Of the two thousand, two hundred and eight passengers and crew aboard *Titanic*, one hundred thirty-three were children.

To acknowledge them, we have a children's gallery at *Titanic Museum Attraction*. It is upstairs, just before the Interactive Gallery, which includes what we refer to as the sloping decks. There are three decks, the last of which is steepest. It is the nearly horizontal slope passengers faced two minutes before *Titanic* sank.

Our young guests are immediately drawn to these sloping decks when they enter the Interactive Gallery, and many of them scramble up even the steepest of the three with the agility of youth and the effervescence of life that causes us adults to sometimes observe them with consternation. The older we get, the more we experience a fleeting envy, the biting pang of loss for our own youth when we, too, were limber and commanded this lithesome energy. Our pelts were glossy, our skin unmarked and supple, and life bubbled within us with the effervescence of the surf.

The other day I was Father Browne again, and I happened to be upstairs near the sloping decks when a smiling young girl of around ten appeared, all prim and fresh in a beige, sleeveless top and pink, pleated skirt shaded with subtle cloud designs. What caught my attention, though, were the cat ears that at first glance appeared to be part of her glossy dark hair. They were a softness of some grey, fuzzy material, edged with dark stripes. The ears themselves were little triangles perched above her head.

She looked up at me, smiling.

"Oh, I do like your cat ears," I said to her.

She smiled and turned to the side, and I laughed. There was a cat's tail of the same fuzzy gray, striped design, looking for all the world a natural part of her. And, of course, she flounced over to the first of the three sloping decks and began to ascend with a true feline grace, looking back at me to see that she still had my attention.

The girl's mother wandered in and smiled up at her daughter. I thought I detected on the mother's face the hint of that same slight wonder for how it is to be a young girl pretending to be a cat and looking so achingly innocent even as this sinewy strength of youth pulses in every twitch of muscle and ripple of her delight.

There is something that surges through our human species in every generation, as though alive. Achingly strong in our youth, it is scary to observe. Its shadow, its signature, is something so stubborn and yet riveted within us with such beauty and promise that those of us who are old enough to be far enough removed to really see it are filled with wonder and dismay.

Sometimes we mistakenly believe it is this fleeting stage of youth that holds the promise and that the enemy is age. I wonder, though, as I watch the children of our own time, the vibrant youth who visit our museum. Certainly, it is true that they are resplendent with this vibrant, lithesome flicker of fragility and promise that we yearn for.

I think, however, that the ache we sometimes feel when we observe these children is a signal of the longing to become. We sense it as we observe this newest generation of children. Our quest, however, our challenge, is to learn to understand who we are as humans, and what it is we are becoming.

Even those of us who are older resonate with this something our species has yet to access or to understand.

Through long experience, we simply accept that we are here, and that the planet will move onward in its stately, perfect course as it glides through its part of the Universe.

One of the most important parts of our experience and urgent mission on this planct is the children.

As my wife and I would begin the ritual at our house for going to bed, the stillness in the house seemed to rise from the corners. The shadow of the darkness crept from corners and hovered near the ceiling. The children found their beds and would lie down and then, before I could go to bed myself, I would hear them calling me with soft, familiar voices.

"Come rub my back."

I would go into the girls' room and knead and rub the back of first one of the girls and then the other. Often, I would rub Alice's back first. She was the more delicate of the two girls, and I could not rub hard or too vigorously. She would say, "Ow, Daddy. You're too rough."

But with Erin, our youngest, I learned to really knead her back and push. If I didn't, she would grumble, "Come on, Daddy. You can do better than that."

And my son, Nick, wanted some powerful kneading of his back.

So that was part of the ritual of putting them to bed. Deep inside of me was this nearly inexpressible love and a primitive certainty that I would protect them. At whatever cost to me, I would. If someone came to the door and tried to harm them, I would become a fighting machine. Something deep within me would rumble up, and I would no doubt yell some guttural shout and attack the predator, the enemy, with every ounce of strength I had.

Perhaps a good deal of why I linger over these thoughts of what we have in common with all who went before is that we are related. From one time or era to another, it is as though on many levels we are connected.

Chapter Sixteen—Childhood Fascinations with Sharks, Father Browne, and Dixie Cups

As our guests enter the first gallery of the museum, the Map Room, they sometimes feel a bit awkward, not quite sure how this is supposed to go. I am delighted when I see that my brief welcome usually sets them at ease.

Often it is a family with children. One of my favorite seasons is summer when the children are out of school, or perhaps Christmas vacation, or Spring Break.

The children come in, sometimes shyly, cautiously. They remind me of scouts, wary and not quite ready to trust. There is an instinctive caution as they discover the lay of the land, so to speak.

But that is why I like to amble over and welcome them, setting the tone with a smile and getting across, if possible, that this is a safe place and one where we can relax and have fun.

Of course, there is a delicate balance between the sense of role play and imagination that we encourage. A fine balance between that and the understanding that the *Titanic* represents a disaster at sea with huge loss of life. It is a celebration of life going forward, even as we recognize the sadness of this event, of what it meant to the people who were so deeply affected by it.

The children who visit our museum bring a heady sense of life. In them is the effervescing surf, as though they are the forerunners of this new generation. Just as the sea rhythmically surges in with that insistent, steady rhythm, so our children come. They are filled with so much which is achingly beautiful: fragile and yet strong.

I walk over to welcome a family just entering the Map Room and encounter a dark-haired little girl wearing a dress of deep, navy blue that reminds me of the outfit Olive Oyl typically wore in Popeye cartoons.

She is hovering behind her parents as they stand at the Map, listening to my presentation. Suddenly, she steps around and looks up with wide eyes.

"Sharks?" she asks. "Were there sharks?"

Directly in front of me as I stand before the Map is an authentic steamer trunk from the *Titanic*. It belonged to a Third Class passenger. We don't know whose it was, but inside that trunk there was a blouse such as a young girl would wear. It is on display upstairs in the children's gallery, and just seeing the reality of that blouse, there is an answering tug within us. We can imagine the girl who wore it, and she is suddenly real, as the children surging through the museum are real.

You never know what our children will do, how they might react. The other day I was walking into the Children's Gallery, dressed as Father Browne. Two blonde-haired children, a brother and a sister, suddenly laughed raucously and pointed at me. I realized that to them, I was a spectacle. Dressed in my priest's cassock and wearing a strange hat with a pom-pom, I must have been strange to them.

At the Map again a few days later, there was a blonde-haired girl. I guessed her age at around five. She was animatedly telling her version of the story of how the ship was exciting and new.

"It sank," she said, gesturing with her fingers pointing down. "And that ruined their vacation."

There are children from other countries speaking in their own languages. Whatever their language, they have this effervescing life and excitement. I was fascinated to see a Swedish family moving slowly, contentedly through the Shipyard Gallery. Their four children were laughing, chattering in Swedish. The youngest one, a little girl in a pink shirt, stood with hands on hips, leaning forward and flipping her hair side-to-side.

On another day, I was emphasizing that any item they see that is in a glass case is authentic, not a replica.

"That trunk, for example," I said, pointing to the steamer trunk near the Map. "It belonged to a Third Class passenger on the *Titanic.* This is her trunk."

A little girl who appeared to be seven or eight years-old tossed her head and said, "He *or* she. We don't know which."

I hadn't yet told them about the young girl's blouse they would see upstairs in the Children's Gallery. I thought it was interesting and charming in its way that this young guest was already thinking in such specific terms and not shy about pointing out what she believed to require more specificity.

One evening, my heart went out to an adolescent girl. She was one of three girls who came over to the Map together and listened intently to my presentation. Afterwards, we were chatting, and I was telling each girl something about the passenger on the boarding pass we give each of our guests.

This onc girl happened to have the boarding pass featuring Margaret Graham, the nineteen-year-old heiress of the *Dixie Cup* fortune.

The girl looked at me shyly.

"Was I cute?" she asked.

There was something in the expression in her eyes and the hesitant way she asked.

"Almost as cute as you," I said.

She and her two friends reminded me of the sometimes achingly awkward adventures of being in transition from childhood to adulthood.

And that is another part of what tugs at this something deep inside when we consider the *Titanic.* Perhaps it is appropriate that we walk this fine line at *Titanic Museum Attraction*, encouraging the role play and delight in the life that *Titanic* represents, the best of our instinctive reach toward the excitement of exploration, discovery, and new achievements in technology. We celebrate even as we respect and deeply feel the tragedy itself, the loss and the anguish passengers and crew endured during that awful night. And that is not to mention the anguish of the families and others who lost loved ones on that ship.

But in so many ways, *Titanic* represents these cycles of our lives, both the joy of riding high, as though propelled in the cusp of a powerful wave during our most exhilarating highs, and the devastating losses we endure as we inevitably deal with tragedies, death, and so much that we do not understand. The *Titanic* takes us through all of that, and we attempt to guide guests to the museum through it, honoring passengers and crew by telling their stories, as we present history and convey the meaning of *Titanic* in all its many facets—its thrill and its devastating loss.

One thing is certain, though. I see in the young ones who visit our museum so much of who we are in any era, in any generation. And there is the sense of life and the flinging forth of each new generation, not unlike the insistent rhythms of the sea.

Chapter Seventeen—Titaniacs

Sometimes we will say to a guest who has a passion for the *Titanic*, "Oh, you are a *Titaniac.*"

That is a complement at *Titanic Museum Attraction*, because it identifies the person as someone like us. All of us here at this world-class museum are ourselves *Titaniacs*. Possibly the biggest qualification for someone to be employed at our museum is having a passion for *Titanic.*

We are always learning: reading, studying various aspects of the ship, its passengers, crew, and all the many small, fascinating details that cause this ship to resonate, to reach out to us even today.

Often, one of our guests will confess to me with a smile that he—or she—has been fascinated with *Titanic* since childhood. And there will be groups of students strolling through, and it is clear from their questions that they have prepared thoroughly, studying the *Titanic* in anticipation of their visit.

I realize that this is a big occasion for them, and I can just feel their sharp minds thinking, processing, in that special, creative state the human mind is capable of when it is most actively challenged and in the process of learning. Often our *Titaniacs* are young, and it can be quite delightful to see them in the throes of their excitement.

A few weeks ago, a teenage girl walked in with her parents. She had braces which made her smile particularly charming, and she had the awkward grace of an adolescent girl who would in a few years be very beautiful. But she was shy until I happened to ask, "Are you excited about touring our museum?"

Somehow those words released what must have been barely contained excitement. She began to dance in a circle, raising her hands.

"Oh yes!" she said, as her parents smiled and chuckled.

The father was shaking his head, nodding.

"She has been looking forward to this for most of the year. It's what she wanted for her birthday. We've come all the way from Chicago."

It is such moments—and there are many of them—that make all of us feel so warm and glad just to be here. Just to have some part in providing an experience that is so memorable and unforgettable for so many of our guests.

And occasionally, just when I have not expected it, something like this girl's excitement will happen, with the realization that this trip to our museum is a major event. Sometimes, there are more subtle clues, such as when these three young children approached the Map with their mother—two girls and a boy.

I noticed that each of them was dressed in nautical blues. The girls wore blue skirts and white blouses with little anchors. The young boy wore navy blue shorts, and a white t-shirt that said *Titanic* Swim Team. That one made me smile. But little things like dress let us know that these families have looked forward to this visit. They have carefully planned.

We feel simultaneously humbled and excited to help them have an unforgettable experience. That is our goal. We may not always succeed. But there is a culture at *Titanic Museum Attraction*, fostered by the wonderful owners, the Joslyns, affectionately known to all of us as Mary and John.

From the time we begin our association with *Titanic Museum Attraction*, we are steeped in this culture of always giving our guests the best. The desire is deeply within us to bring the *Titanic* to life for each of our guests, who have so many questions.

A man wearing a visor with artificial wooly dark hair erupting from the top, asks, “Why didn’t they have enough lifeboats?”

Some of our guests preface questions like that with a shy suggestion that it is a dumb one.

“But there are no dumb questions here,” I tell them.

The question might come from the man in the dark visor and woolly hair, or from the shy girl who is wearing a scarf around her neck in the style of Gryffindor, one of the student houses in the Harry Potter series.

Whether it is the man or that shy girl who loved to feel near the camaraderie of the Harry Potter series, we continue to be mystified as to why there were not enough lifeboats.

And, of course, today, we can begin to tick off answers on our fingers. The fingers of one hand will do it. It might be that only three fingers will be enough.

One, of course, is that nearly everyone believed the *Titanic* to be unsinkable, due to newspaper coverage.

“No, they did not have enough lifeboats, and the lifeboats they did have were not filled to capacity. Certainly, the first ones were not. Even after *Titanic* struck the iceberg, passengers did not believe the ship was sinking."

In fact, there was an atmosphere of amusement, of excited fun.

"First Class passengers were reportedly having snowball fights with pieces of the iceberg that had been sheered off and fallen onto the boat deck when the *Titanic* scraped along the sharp edge of that iceberg."

People generally chuckle when I tell them that some of them were dropping pieces of the ice into their drinks and joking about it.

"In the first half hour or so after the ship struck the iceberg, many of the First Class passengers felt that it was an amusing diversion, a story that would later be entertaining for their friends."

Another reason there weren't enough lifeboats is that the law governing *Titanic* in 1912 was written when ships were much smaller. The law advised that the most lifeboats a ship was required to have was sixteen.

Later, the *White Star Line* expressed consternation with criticism that *Titanic* did not have enough lifeboats. *Titanic* had twenty lifeboats, more than maritime law required at that time.

A third reason there were not enough lifeboats was interference from *White Star Line* director Bruce Ismay. His logic seems strange to us today. Ismay argued that passengers would think *White Star Line* feared the ship would sink if there were so many lifeboats cluttering the boat deck.

Ismay's insistence that there be fewer lifeboats countermanded ship's architect Thomas Andrews, whose plans included a full complement of lifeboats.

We delight in questions, though. Whether they come from curious children or their parents, we are delighted to deepen their understanding of the Titanic and how we are, all of us, connected with that ship and the excited individuals who sailed on her with such hopes for the future.

Chapter Eighteen—Titanic and Changing Attitudes Toward Women

Dominating the Memorial Room is a wall with the names of each person known to have been onboard the *Titanic*. Names are grouped by class. There is a panel for Crew, and there is a panel for First Class, Second Class, and Third Class passengers. On each panel, names are divided into two groups: those who survived and those who perished.

Often, I will find our guests shaking their heads at what they see as the unfairness of class distinction. At first glance, it appears that First Class and Second Class passengers fared better. Certainly not as many perished in these classes.

By far, the largest numbers to perish were Third Class and Crew.

With the crew, it is assumed that the passengers must be allowed to go first. Crew members who survived included twenty of the twenty-three stewardesses. They were women and were allowed on the lifeboats due to the code of chivalry. Women and children first.

Other crew members survived because they were assigned to lifeboats. Someone had to know how to row. We needed strong, hearty men to row. Perhaps that is why the highest percentage of crew members to survive were the firemen, the hearty men who shoveled coal into the furnaces. They were among the strongest men on board and would be likely choices to man the lifeboats.

It is true that far fewer perished among First and Second Class passengers. However, this had little to do with money. In fact, some of the wealthiest men on the ship did not survive.

Two factors were responsible for fewer First Class or Second Class passengers perishing. One factor is that there were far fewer First and Second Class passengers. The second, and most important, factor is related to this Code of Chivalry. It was women and children first, and the men in these two classes were reluctant to board one of the lifeboats.

Society of that era took the Code of Chivalry seriously. If a gentleman boarded a lifeboat onboard ship, he would bring shame upon himself and his family. He behaved dishonorably by the standards of that day. It was assumed that he had taken the place of a woman or a child.

Most men who were in First Class and Second Class did what was deeply woven into the expectations of that day. They stayed onboard. Even John Jacob Astor, the wealthiest man aboard, did not survive. And Astor was extolled in newspaper accounts published after the sinking, praised as an ideal Edwardian Period man. He was cool under pressure, did all he could to help women and children board lifeboats. In other words, he behaved admirably and did his duty as a man.

At any rate, if you look at those who perished in First Class or Second Class, you will find that mostly men perished here. The survivors in these classes were—for the most part—women and children.

Today, however, the idea of a Code of Chivalry has not survived. Margaret Brown was right when she predicted that if women began to achieve equality with men, the idea of women and children first to the lifeboats would be gone.

The women I chat with at *Titanic Museum Attraction* smile when I tell them that men today have no qualms with telling me quite openly that they would feel no shame about taking a lifeboat.

Many of the men I encounter in the Memorial Room have this good natured, locker room kind of presence in the world. They smile and shake their heads, as if to say, "Well, I hate it, but yes, I would be climbing over those women to get into a lifeboat."

At least that is the attitude of many of these guys. They're not bad people, and I'm sure they have their own sense of honor. But things have changed today, and most notably have changed regarding the status, the expectations, the aspirations of women. And that is a good thing, surely.

But isn't it interesting that in that time, in that era, the limiting expectations of society toward women were to be challenged, and a number of women onboard *Titanic* were leading the charge. These would include Margaret Tobin Brown, and the social activist Helen Candee.

Speaking of Helen Candee, she was an early riser, and she liked to go out to the bow of the ship, fill her lungs with that bracing sea air, and sometimes fling wide her arms. It is said that the scene in that now iconic movie with Leonardo DiCaprio and Kate Winslet as Jack and Rose was based on Helen Candee. You know the one, where Jack and Rose are at the bow, and Rose leans out, arms open, Jack steadying her.

Interesting to me, though, the changes that occur in our attitudes, and especially in our assumptions about who we are and what we are becoming, as well as what it means to be a person of honor.

We move forward, always connected in any era. And we must come together. There is always this deep, ferocious urge of procreation. On one level, that is the one defining characteristic, and is the reason we surge forward, flinging our DNA, our genetic material, from one generation to another.

However, there is more. Much more, and as we consider such alluring, fascinating incidents as the *Titanic,* we must sift and become sensitive to these other, somewhat less visible parts of who we are and what it is that drives us. These elusive, challenging *things* that are near us, within us, tugging at this indefinable *something deep within.*

I would suggest that the *Titanic* is like a magnet, in a sense. Something about it draws, tugs, animates this elusive, indefinable something that is our most unexamined, even our trivialized, part. It is there, hidden, and it is the one thing that summons us, draws us in every age.

Chapter Nineteen—Last Remnants of Two Passengers

There are physical parts of two passengers on display in *Titanic Museum* Attraction. Isn't it interesting that we can sense how people were in the parts of themselves that survive in our museum? There are several of these that seem strange at first. For example, I sometimes stand in the Third Class hallway and look at Selena Cook's tooth. Yes, it is a part of Selena, who was a youthful twenty-two-year-old woman in 1912.

The tooth appears to be a molar, and it reminds me of our humanness. We are such interesting, fragile creatures in any era. Hostages to these biological forms. But how interesting and touching to glimpse the actual tooth of a young lady who was very much alive and in her prime upon the *Titanic.*

Selena Cook had only recently married, but she was traveling to visit relatives in New York. Her new husband was not with her on the *Titanic.* And here is her tooth. She suffered a toothache while aboard *Titanic.* She had the tooth extracted and, as a survivor, kept it always in the little box which once held her wedding ring. Rather strange, isn't it?

It does reveal a subtle glimpse of her humanness, though. Such artifacts make us feel close to the passengers onboard and help us feel connected. We have so much in common. We are similar in our own daily existence. We all have teeth. Most of us have had a toothache and suffered anxious visits to the dentist.

Here is something I hadn't thought of in many years, but Selena Cook's tooth reminds me. When I was in third grade, long ago, way back in the mid-twentieth century, doctors believed it best to remove tonsils from children's throats, and it was not unusual for the children to ask for their extracted tonsils and keep them afterwards.

In the early Spring of my year in Third Grade, lined up in a long row along the window sill in our classroom, were glass jars. Some held the first yellow daffodils, beautiful flowers. Others, however, were filled with formaldehyde. Each of the smelly formaldehyde jars displayed two lumpy, stubbly tonsils. Yes, there was a time when we kept such things. Baby teeth, tonsils. Perhaps some people still do today. I used to tease my children, when they were young, offering them some of my fingernail clippings to cherish and pretending to be hurt when they twitched their noses and said, "Oh, gross, Daddy."

But we are all inescapably human in every age. Connections, you know. And Selena Cook's tooth reminds us that we all have teeth, must daily tend to them, and use them to gnaw the food, which is another of the activities we constantly participate in. Always the routines, the necessities of human life.

And how about this for another oddity of the *Titanic* era:

It was considered a token of affection to send a clipping of your hair along with a letter to someone you cherished.

At *Titanic Museum Attraction*, you might want to look for the authentic letter First Class passenger Alfred Rowe writes to his wife, whom he obviously adores. He addresses her as his *dear girl.* He unveils his honest feelings. More, he expresses his adoration by enclosing some of himself.

Displayed with the letter is a tuft of his moustache hair, delicately tied with a little thread. Strange to us today, perhaps. However, what an intimate way to share, along with your written thoughts, a literal part of yourself. Reading this letter in his own firm hand, we get the sense that his wife is the love of his life. Rowe's letter is another endearing reminder that these were real people with depth and emotion.

Another element of Rowe's letter, however, is a departure from most passenger letters. Passengers usually express delight and amazement when describing the *Titanic.* They can't say enough about the wonder, the incredible adventure of this ship. Rowe, however, is less than pleased.

"My dearest," he writes, "she is too big. You can't find your way about, and it takes too long to get anywhere."

Rowe had immigrated to the United States from England and was a successful rancher in Texas.

Thanks to the tradition of that time, though, we today have an actual part of the man himself, cattle rancher Alfred Rowe, who sported a mustache. Some of the man himself, on display at our museum.

Like most First Class gentlemen, Alfred Rowe did not survive. The Code of Chivalry, you remember, was a stern, no nonsense expectation that a gentleman would allow the women and children first to the lifeboats. The expectation was that a proper Edwardian Period gentleman would not board a lifeboat in circumstances such as this one.

There were too few lifeboats, only twenty. If every lifeboat had been loaded to capacity—which they weren't—

fewer than half of the two thousand, two hundred and eight passengers and crew could have been rescued.

Note that Rowe's letter was mailed from Queenstown, Ireland, *Titanic's* last stop before heading on to America. Any letter not transferred from the ship before Queenstown never reached its destination. Such letters are lost somewhere beneath the North Atlantic, disintegrating in a mailbag which is now two-and-a-quarter miles down, where *Titanic* herself is becoming increasingly brittle and is not expected to outlast this century.

We feel the loss of a magnificent ship even as we feel a connection with passengers and crew. Our artifacts resonate, call to something within us as we consider them, understanding that we and *Titanic* passengers and crew are kindred spirits. In their stories, their possessions, we see much of who we are in our own era, as well as much of what humans have always been.

Chapter Twenty—Children and Their Stuffed Animals

On this day, a Monday, I am Father Francis Browne, the Jesuit Priest-in-training who captured the only photographs of life onboard *Titanic.* We are steady but slow enough that I can greet guests personally as they begin their tour.

Stepping into the Map Room from Admissions is a family of three: mother, father, and a dark-haired little girl with a stuffed animal clasped under one arm. It appears to be a cat.

When I approach, the little girl looks up at me with concern, her eyes flicking to my black cassock, then up to the priestly hat upon my head. It is called a biretta. It has a pom-pom on top. From the sash around my waist dangles a cross attached to rosary beads.

I smile, open my hands in a gesture of greeting.

"Welcome to your self-guided tour," I say. "We are delighted that you are here."

I am happy to see them smile and relax as I show them the numbers on the far wall which begin the audio tour on their handheld devices. The dark-haired little girl trots immediately to the display panel in front of a large diagram of the *Titanic.*

"Good," I say, smiling at the parents. "She has found what immediately attracts our young guests. The red buttons are irresistible. And when you press one of the buttons, it lights up an area of the ship, and you can read on the panel what that area is showing you."

As I chat with these guests, showing them the authentic deck chair in the first display case, I can feel the familiar sense of connection between us wash over me.

I can feel in these families this mesmerizing sense that we are, all of us, connected. There are markers, elements that link us. Is it simply our DNA? We bear the same genetic triggers that define much of who we are. But what is this *other* that I sense as I watch the children?

At the Map, the parents address their daughter as Cindy. She appears to be six-years-old, and now she is cradling her cat, which is light gray with black stripes.

"Did you know," I ask her, "that there were children onboard *Titanic* much like you? And many of them carried animal friends. Yours is a cat, isn't it?"

Cindy smiles and pushes her cat toward me, her arms outstretched.

"Is it a boy cat or a girl cat?" I ask.

"It's a girl cat," she says, smiling.

I am amazed with her eyes, and with the eyes of all these children who visit us. Whatever the season, there they are, looking up at me. Such clear, fresh pigments. But there is also this difficult-to-describe life. It is something that transcends and has much to do with this mystery of who we are and what we are becoming.

Cindy shyly tells me that her cat's name is Tabitha Sue.

"But I call her Tabby," she says. "Want to pat her? Scratch behind her ears. She likes that."

I feel honored in the trust she shows me. I smile as I scratch the cat, Tabby, behind the ears.

Often, though, young children enter the Map Room, take one look at me swathed in my black cassock and strange hat and become very still, like little animals instinctively going quiet, perhaps to escape the notice of a predator. I usually succeed in convincing them that our museum is a safe place, and that I am not what my own children used to refer to on TV shows as a *bad man*—someone they must be wary of.

And perhaps for all of us an initial uneasiness is amplified here at our museum, because lying beneath the wonder of this ship and the triumph it represented for its era is the pall of death, the sudden thrusting of many hundreds of fragile humans into the unthinkable—forced in an instant to have all the warmth and security of the safest, most splendid ship in the world ripped away. And there we all are, our worst fears unfolding about us in the fear, the chaos, the shrieks and groaning of the steel under terrible stress as the ship is tearing itself apart beneath us.

And Father Browne, a priest swathed in a black cassock and wearing a strange black hat, may at first seem imposing. After all, priests perform last rites and are thus associated with death. Also, there is their association with confessions and our perception that they channel God's knowledge of, and disapproval of, our guilt and sin.

Chapter Twenty-one—Father Browne's Photographs

So yes, though there is much that enchants us about the *Titanic*, underlying it all is the lurid, darksome grimace of impending disaster, death, and confrontation with what is out there that we know and live with.

And yet there is something remotely fascinating, teasing us with the shivery dread of allowing ourselves to imagine what that night was like for passengers and crew. Even as we consider it, we can feel relieved that we are not there, except in imagination. It draws something, tugs so many deeply driven parts of us. Titillates, frightens, and fascinates.

As I've mentioned, though, I immediately try to put our guests at ease as they step into our first gallery, the Map Room, welcoming them with genuine pleasure and pointing out their first opportunity to use the audio players they were handed in Admissions. And when they arrive at the big Map, I assure them that I am not really a priest.

"No, I am representing an actual passenger who was on the *Titanic*," I say. "He was a Jesuit priest-in-training who loved photography."

And that is why we are honoring Father Francis Browne.

"Father Browne took a set of wonderful photographs during the brief time he was on the ship, and you will get to see them. We have a gallery to display them for you."

Interesting that our guests noticeably relax when I confess that I am not really a priest. It isn't that they have been all that anxious, just a little wary of me. And I can see them shift into a more relaxed, easy attitude when I explain about Father Browne, and that I am only pretending to be him.

"I always had a love of photography," I tell them as I transition into my Father Browne presentation. "I believe my interest in photography began when I was only a boy. My uncle bought me my very first camera when I was ten."

And I tell them how exciting that was, to be only ten and receive a camera at a time when these small, portable cameras were just becoming available.

"Since my parents had passed away, my uncle was like a father to me. He would often purchase things for me."

"He bought the camera when I was ten. But then, years later, he really outdid himself. He is the one who bought my First Class ticket upon the maiden voyage of the R.M.S. *Titanic.*"

Sometimes I will describe a little of how exciting that was.

"You possibly have no idea," I say, "what it meant to be handed a ticket for this ship, *Titanic.* Imagine someone coming up to you and handing you a pass for a new, amazing space shuttle that will take you and others on a voyage to the moon, where you will orbit that celestial body, glimpsing our fragile, beautiful earth, and experience a closeup view of the moon."

"*Titanic* for its day was the adventure of the new technology. It represented the future and was nearly like science fiction for 1912. The experience of being on that ship was a tremendous adventure."

"From the time I boarded *Titanic*," I tell our guests, "I was taking photographs of everything and everybody."

"I even got a picture of Captain Smith, and it appears to be the only photograph we have of Captain Smith on board *Titanic*."

Many of our guests naturally wonder how these incredible photographs survived. And it appears to be one of those fortunate coincidences. Something like a coincidence, anyway. Some guests suggest that it must have been divine intervention, and I think we could certainly make a case for that.

Here is more of my presentation to our guests.

"The First Class ticket my uncle purchased for me had a limitation. It was only for the first day of the voyage—from Southampton, England to Queenstown, Ireland. I was delighted to have the opportunity to be on the ship, however briefly."

Father Browne was supposed to depart the ship at Queenstown.

"However, I was offered the opportunity to stay on the ship for the entire voyage, all the way to New York City."

I turn and gesture to the big Map, which is immediately behind me. A row of red L.E.D. lights traces the path from Queenstown, dipping gradually to the South as they edge across the Atlantic toward New York. The lights stop at a round, red plastic disc that marks the collision with the iceberg.

"I met this wonderful couple during my brief stay on the ship," I tell our guests. "I guess we had much in common. We chatted away that whole afternoon."

And in conversation, Father Browne tells them how his uncle had bought his First Class ticket, but it was only as far as Queenstown. The couple was disappointed to hear that Father Browne would be leaving the ship the next morning.

"Father Browne," they said. "Surely you can't leave us. We won't have anyone to talk to if you leave the ship."

So the couple offers to pay to have Father Browne's ticket extended.

"You'll be with us, all the way to New York. And then we will buy you a First Class ticket for your return to Ireland."

Father Browne was excited for the opportunity. However, since he was a Jesuit priest-in-training, he was required to obtain permission. He telegraphed his superior, but the reply was unambiguous.

Get off that ship immediately!

So Father Browne disembarked at Queenstown, taking his exposed film with him, which he later developed.

Divine intervention? Very possibly. Some accounts have it that Father Browne's superior later said that he had prayed about the request to stay onboard and had the strongest sense that Father Browne should leave the ship.

Had Father Browne stayed onboard, he almost certainly would not have accepted a place on a lifeboat; he and his film would have sunk with the ship. Fortunately, the film survived, the photographs are incredible, professional, and as sharp and clear as though they are recent. These are the only photographs in the world of life onboard *Titanic*, as far as we know.

Chapter Twenty-two—Women and Children First

So, what was this tradition referred to as the *Code of Chivalry*?

It was taken seriously in that era, the era of the *Titanic*. It led to that now famous phrase: *women and children first* to the lifeboats.

It was something we just wouldn't have thought about or challenged in 1912, though Margaret Tobin Brown, later known as the Unsinkable Molly Brown, had the foresight to warn women that if they succeeded in obtaining the right to vote, to own property, to enter professions that had been reserved only for men, the *Code of Chivalry* would be no more.

"Fair is fair, and don't think that this *women-and-children first* attitude won't change if we begin to obtain equality with men."

That is a paraphrase of what Margaret Tobin Brown advised other women who had begun to break through what we sometimes refer to as the glass ceiling.

I find it interesting now that Margaret Brown was right. Today, women have made great strides, compared to then, and the *Code of Chivalry* has quietly disappeared. Of course, many women would argue that they have more catching up to do, particularly in salaries. However, most male guests at our museum tell me they'd feel no reluctance about boarding lifeboats in a situation similar to the *Titanic*.

Historically, women have long been treated unfairly, misused, and today things are changing. There are challenges, and society is beginning to listen; whereas, even a few years ago, society tended not to listen.

Perhaps it is necessary that we begin to see ourselves differently. We have this sense of who we are and what we are becoming. Seldom, however, do we see ourselves as lifeforms upon a planet, sprays of genetic material being flung forward from one generation to the next.

Some might ask, what is the possible use of seeing ourselves as mere genetic material stubbornly flung forward from one generation into the next?

When we think of the *Titanic*, we think of a major shipwreck, a disaster, and certainly it was. But there is also this idea, this insistence—touted, practically turned into an opera, a major production, as the culture of that day proclaimed that the ship was unsinkable.

God Himself could not sink this ship.

At the Map, we usually note that the statement indicates the pride, the haughty attitudes of the culture of that day.

Our guests sum it up well. I remember a man with a bushy black beard who looked as though he could have worked as one of the firemen in the *Titanic* boiler room, that hot, sweaty area where hundreds of men tended the one hundred fifty-nine furnaces scattered throughout the huge boilers. There were twenty-nine boilers, each one three-stories tall.

But this man with his muscular arms and bushy beard wore a blue-and-white striped shirt and faded blue jeans. He stepped toward me. I was portraying Father Browne on that day, and he leaned across the panel with its round, red buttons and its timeline, tracing the days of the voyage, beginning in Southampton and touching on stops in Cherbourg, France and Queenstown, Ireland.

The man was holding the hand of a little girl who was cradling a fuzzy puppy as though it were a precious friend. A stuffed puppy, I should say. But the bearded man locked eyes with me and kept leaning nearer, his upper body leaning over that panel, and there was something urgent about the expression in his eyes.

When he spoke, his voice was soft, his words quiet and spoken as one who would convey some important private message meant just for me to hear.

"As a priest," he said, "would you say that God really did sink that ship?"

And really, I don't know. I mean, who can say? But I have decided that we can say one thing about it with certainty.

"I believe," I said, "that whenever we become so arrogant that we are capable of saying *God Himself cannot sink this ship*, we are setting ourselves up for a big fall."

The man nodded and glanced down at his little girl.

"I don't want her to think of God that way," he said. "I don't want her to have this idea that God is—what's the word? Help me. There is a word . . ."

"Vindictive?" I offered.

"Yeah, that's it. I don't want her to be afraid of God."

I nodded and smiled.

"It is usually us," I said. "We in our arrogance bring these things on ourselves."

And from there the little girl, who I learned was Susan, began helping her puppy to push the red buttons, and we smiled and just enjoyed her fascination with seeing the little L.E.D. lights begin to trace the path of *Titanic* from Southampton, to Cherbourg, to Queenstown and then on toward our destination, which was New York City.

Chapter Twenty-three—Then and Now: Our Unending Fight for Survival

It was a different time, another era, and the early twentieth century was particularly harsh for crew members of a ship in the aftermath of a sinking.

Upstairs in the museum, in the Interactive Gallery, a *White Star Line* postcard attests with a single, handwritten line to the harshness of what it was like to lose a husband or a family member. Of course, it is terrible to lose someone you love. That brings the world crashing down.

But this one postcard, a remnant from that time, suggests the cruelty of what it meant for the families. This postcard is addressed to a Mrs. Mischellany, and it has a single line.

Regret your husband not saved.

Often, I pause before that display case and stare at this card, feeling some of the pain and the suffocating sense of despair this woman must have experienced as she found that small postcard among her mail. Just a single line. Five grim words that represent the collapse of her world.

That single postcard represents a part of the disaster we may not fully comprehend today. Yes, we understand that two-thirds of those onboard *Titanic* perished. Each one of these lives was precious. Individuals with hopes, dreams, many of them children, the parents of children. Entire families such as the Goodwin family.

I mention the Goodwin family because we have a family portrait displayed outside the Third Class room and again in the Children's Gallery upstairs. A mother, father, and five children—three boys and two girls—posing for this photograph. None of them survived, perhaps because of the tradition of separating Third Class males and females.

The women and children would have rooms on one end of the ship; the boys and men would have rooms on the other end. We believe the Goodwin family waited to board lifeboats until they were all together, and the lifeboats were gone before they could find one another, if in fact they ever did.

It is sad to stand before the Third Class panel in the Memorial Room and find the Goodwin family among the many who perished. Their names take up nearly two lines.

However devastating the loss of individual lives, there is the terrible loss for surviving family members. Mrs. Mischellany, for example, not only lost her husband, but what was most likely her only source of income. The impact on lives, terrible as the loss of a loved one is, often meant devastating, ruinous consequences to families who may have lost their primary breadwinner in this disaster.

Here we see the compassion of Margaret Tobin Brown, later known as the Unsinkable Molly Brown. Perhaps she understood the ruinous financial consequences more than any other First Class passenger. She and her husband had themselves been poor, scratching out a living. Mr. Brown discovered a new technique that allowed the owners of a mine to strike a vein of gold that would have been inaccessible without Mr. Brown's idea. The Browns were suddenly quite wealthy.

Following the *Titanic* disaster, Margaret Brown began a fund to help those who had been left in terrible financial circumstances due to the sinking. Thanks to her efforts, there was a safety net available to families who otherwise would have had nothing.

That innocent postcard addressed to Mrs. Mischellany is a reminder of the stark reality of the time. The *White Star Line*, the company that managed the *Titanic*, was under no obligation to do anything more than inform the family of the death of a crew member. It is likely that *White Star Line* management felt they were going beyond what the law required when they troubled themselves to send a card.

Our museum guests are even more shocked to learn that family members of the *Titanic* musicians, who courageously played music until the bitter end, received a card that requested they pay a sum equivalent to the cost of the uniform the deceased musician was wearing.

Yes, how outrageous and unfeeling it seems to us, and yet these cards are evidence of the harshness of the era. Protections had not yet been put into place for victims of disasters. Business owners were generally under no obligation to their employees, even when employees died as a result of some failure of the business to protect them.

As I consider these cruel responses, I experience uneasiness concerning our predicament as humans. We search for what we have in common in every age, which is our unending quest for survival. In every moment, there is this survival urge. And even when I am at the museum, strolling through the galleries, interacting with our guests,

I am engaged in survival. Though I love working here, the reason I sought out the job is to earn money necessary to support my family.

I dislike referring to this as a job. It seems disrespectful. And when I am here, interacting with the guests, using story to help us experience the *Titanic*'s era, I feel connected to two eras: the Edwardian Period and now. That is part of why this rises above a mere job. We speak of jobs as work. Jobs come with the idea that we are captured, imprisoned, forced to labor in order to be paid.

What happens at *Titanic Museum Attraction,* however, is not like that. Through story and imagination, we transcend time, and we move out into that era until we feel we are there. In many respects, it is not a job. But yes, I am there as part of the human enigma, the necessity of acquiring the wherewithal to support myself, my family. That is one part of survival.

When I pause with one of our guests to consider the postcard so impersonally mailed to Mrs. Mischellany, I can sense the harshness, the despair. In one sense, we are safe from the terror of the night of the sinking and immune from the desperate, cold fear and frustration Mrs. Mischellany must have felt. However, we can identify with Mrs. Mischellany and all who face the uncertainty of life and the dangers that beset us here in what—even now—is an unending fight for survival.

Chapter Twenty-four—More on How Titanic Speaks to Our Human Predicament

There is something here with us in our own time, when we pause to consider bits of detritus from the past such as a letter or card, written in cursive script, the ink a little smeared. And we must employ our own empathy and capacity for imagining how it must have been for the recipient.

When I do such an excellent job of imagining that I am there in that moment, it is as though I am standing near Mrs. Mischellany as she discovers this impersonal card. I hear the sharp intake of her breath as she absorbs the full meaning of five words scrawled onto that card: *Regret your husband not saved.* She lives in a city, and there is the clatter of a few automobiles, and perhaps at that time there was the rattle of the harnesses that hitched horses to wagons with iron shod wheels.

But mostly this is the indifference of the city that is all around her. It is the commerce that will continue, impervious to her grief, rumbling on like some machine. And perhaps in any time in our history, even thousands of years ago, there was for that ancient era the din of whatever passed for routine life and people with their own concerns. And one fragile, vulnerable human who endures the agony of loss, of a riveting fear for what being alone and without sustenance in an indifferent world feels like.

But on this afternoon at *Titanic Museum Attraction*, there is something like a bump as I am released from my vivid imaginings of what it must have been like for Mrs.

Mischellany. I am here. It is the experience of awakening from a dream with an intense relief of realizing the dream was so real, and yet it was only a dream. Or if I had been there through vivid imagination, I have now escaped, the way a time traveler might rescue himself from danger by pressing a lever on his time machine and easing away from the moment that was so harsh, so dangerous, escaping whatever dilemma he was in.

And I'll have to tell you, just to be honest, that I believe we are all travelers in time. Perhaps that is why museums fascinate us, for when we are there, we slip sideways for a while and discover that we have, even for a few moments, travelled. We are for a little while edging away from our own time into another, and yet we have the security of knowing we are safe in our own world. At least we cannot be robbed of what protections we have in our own time.

But of course, there is this truth that we must learn to live with. In every waking moment it moves within us and travels with us. It is the frustrating certainty that, regardless of what happens to us in this world, in this era, in this softness of the planet with its fragile atmosphere and rhythms, much is the same as in any era. But what is certain, what ultimately unites us, is that we are destined to grow old, to become weak, and expire. It is one of the realities we learn to accept.

The *Titanic* disaster tugs at this place within us, for always near that place is this reluctant understanding that we are all in this predicament of life, embracing the vigorous energy of what it is to live, to form families, relationships, and what can be the exhilarating experience of adventure and hope for the future. But in thc *Titanic* disaster we see—played out in a matter of minutes—the entire panoply of our predicament.

There is this ship, said to be the safest ever built, magnificent, and a monument to our constant attempts to design environments that protect us from the savagery of nature. Passengers feel secure, only to be stripped of that security in mere moments. The shift is immediate and horrifying. From the warmth and apparent safety of the ship, they find themselves standing unprotected and frightened in the cold elements outside with the brilliant universe sketched across the sky. All those stars. No moonlight that night, and yet such amazing stars.

And we realize, those of us who remain on the ship, unable to step into a lifeboat, we realize with that deep bite of fear that all that we had worked so hard for, all the protections and plans, are all in a moment gone. We are only moments away from that death that has always been a distant reality but now is right here. And what a staggering, devastating moment that is, so suddenly to have come.

And yes, a big part of that tug we feel lies here, in how the *Titanic* disaster resonates so deeply within us, tugging and shaking this most basic fear—the inevitability of our eventual death, regardless of wealth or station in life. There comes the stark, awful moment that Mrs. Mischellany feels as she examines the five words on that impersonal card.

And it is what so many felt as loved ones vanished with a terrible swiftness, and those left behind were left in fear, distress, and the bitter taste of being penniless and alone in a world that would go rumbling on, regardless. Such a frightening, devastating circumstance.

Chapter Twenty-five—Last Heroes, and the Experience of Titanic

With the *Titanic,* we have the society, the culture of 1912 celebrating *the* achievement of that era. Part of what thrilled passengers on the maiden voyage was the sense of riding the crest of a wave, the evidence of human brilliance, and the promise of an exciting future.

They dutifully held worship services on the Sunday morning of April 14th. There were services for Protestants and there were services for Catholics. We know that Father Thomas Byles presented a service that emphasized that each one of us needs a spiritual lifeboat. Of course, he had no idea that before that day ended, all passengers and crew would be in desperate need of a physical lifeboat because the unthinkable had happened. The great *Titanic* had struck an iceberg and was doomed to sink.

Titanic Museum Attraction includes a tribute to the men of God who were onboard *Titanic.* It is in the Memorial Room, where our guests can discover the fate of the person whose story is presented on their boarding pass. Two thousand, two hundred and eight onboard the ship. Only seven hundred and twelve survived, which is approximately a third of those on the ship.

We call these ministers and priests the spiritual heroes of *Titanic.* There were nine men of God, and only one chose to board a lifeboat. Each of them was serious about his calling and therefore felt it necessary to stay and help the many who could not board a lifeboat. Around fifteen hundred passengers and crew were left to endure the frightening final minutes of the ship, knowing the lifeboats had all been launched and that they were likely living the final minutes of their lives.

It all happened so quickly. From the time the *Titanic* scraped along the edge of that massive iceberg, only two hours and forty minutes passed before the ship shuddered, shrieked with twisting steel, and was pulled under by the weight of all the water flooding the ship.

I love to hear Lowell Lytle, official Captain of *Titanic Museum Attraction* in Pigeon Forge, tell the story of Rev. John Harper, one of the nine spiritual heroes of *Titanic.*

"When the *Titanic* began to sink," Lowell says, "Rev. Harper's faith was put to the test. That Baptist minister ran around the decks shouting *women, children, and unsaved people, get on board the lifeboats!"*

Lowell speaks with a deep, resonant voice. He is a master storyteller, and he captivates our guests when he visits our museum.

"He even took off his lifejacket and gave it to a man who was not a believer in Jesus Christ. He thought that might give the man more time to prepare his soul for eternity, because eternity was about to happen."

It's a true story, beautifully told in the book *Titanic's Last Hero,* by Moody Adams.

When I shared with Lowell that I was writing a book about my experiences with guests at our museum, Lowell was happy to share some of his own.

"One time," Lowell told me, "while walking through the Memorial Room, I saw an elderly lady bent over and kissing a name on that memorial board."

"When she straightened, I asked her, 'Why did you do that?' "

"She said, 'That was my father. He was a crew member on the *Titanic*, and he survived.' "

Lowell embodies the essence and the spirit of *Titanic* as well as the passion museum crew members have for the ship and for sharing with our guests. Tall, with a deep, resonant voice, Lowell mesmerizes our guests with his own fascinating experiences and deep knowledge of *Titanic*. Our guests are transfixed when they meet him on the Captain's Bridge.

Perhaps most fascinating are his first-hand accounts of what it was like on his dive to the *Titanic*. As he points out, there are many more astronauts who have gone into outer space than anyone who has dived on the *Titanic*.

Lowell also holds our guests absolutely enthralled with some of his own adventures in a long, full life. He still enjoys rollercoasters and has even tried bungie jumping.

His comment on his bungie jumping experience always makes me laugh along with the guests.

"If you ever want to experience what it's like to commit suicide and live to tell about it, try bungie jumping!"

Lowell loves interacting with guests visiting the Captain's Bridge.

"I believe some of the most enjoyable times that I have while being on the Bridge occur when I see young people who are usually around seven years of age darting back and forth touching different items looking as if they were seeing Christmas presents. I can usually tell if they are *Titaniacs* when they see me and immediately hide behind their mother's skirt. This is all of a sudden very real to them."

"I remember one boy in particular. "I asked his parents, does he know much about the *Titanic*?"

"'Oh yes!' they exclaim. 'He is obsessed about it. That's why we're here. We have driven hundreds of miles just to please him.' "

"And I said to this boy, 'Come over here. I've got something I want to show you.' Then I explain to him and to those who are listening about my dive to the Titanic in the year 2000, picking up artifacts."

"One of those artifacts," I say, "is a First Class window. When we resurfaced and removed the window from the basket, little pieces of rust from the metal frame of that window fell off. Little pieces of the *Titanic*!"

"I told the boy to hold out his hand, and I press a few of the rust pieces into his palm. I tell him that very few people will ever hold actual pieces of *Titanic*."

"You should see the expression on his face. I wish I had a camera to capture it."

"Once in a while, I will glance up and look at the parents of other such children and see smiles and tears knowing that their child is enjoying this to the fullest!"

"You just can't put a price on that."

Lowell Lytle, our beloved Captain, represents the best of what we all try to do at *Titanic Museum Attraction*, which is to help our many guests experience the fascinating history and aura of the great *Titanic*.

Chapter Twenty-six—True Love: Ida and Isador Straus

Our crew members often refer to the *Titanic Museum Attraction* as *The Ship*. For us, it is a place that becomes the *Titanic* through our identification with the passengers and crew and through the engagement of our museum guests. There are so many moments when, through story, we are there in that era, experiencing the *Titanic.*

One of the most powerful parts of who we are in any era is our capacity for love. We see this not only in romantic love, but also in the love of family members, particularly in parents and their children—both on the *Titanic* and in our museum guests.

There is a heightened awareness of how fleeting life is when tragedy strikes. In the routines of the everyday, we often take precious life and relationships for granted. However, when all of that is threatened, then we have this heightened awareness of how fleeting, how fragile our lives are. One fascination of the *Titanic* is how the disaster sharpens our awareness of who we are and causes us to focus on the big picture.

Ida and Isidor Straus represent genuine love and a refusal to be parted from one another. Their story deeply affects guests who visit the First Class sitting room, which we have dedicated to Ida and Isidor.

Our guests experience a strong reaction, an identification, because the Straus story does pull at something deep within us: our capacity for love, and our identification with two people who have become such inseparable companions that they refuse to be parted.

The First Class sitting room is beautiful with its twenty-four-karat gold leaf trim, its electric fireplace, the comfortable Edwardian Period tables, chairs, writing desk. But there are also framed photographs of Ida and Isidor Straus.

One photograph captures them when they were young, probably taken to commemorate their engagement, or it might have been taken soon after their wedding. I like to point out to our guests, though, how they seem a little stiff and self-conscious in this photograph. Their love has not yet matured.

There is a second photograph taken many decades later in which they are deeply comfortable with one another. We can sense the depth of their love that has grown, matured. They feel blended.

Our guests do respond to the depth of that love. The story is told and retold and causes us to feel this warmth and identification with them. It begins with Ida's refusal to take a lifeboat seat if Isidor will not be joining her.

I often have the honor of portraying the writer and military historian, Col. Archibald Gracie. We know from the reports of survivors that Col. Gracie offered to ask a deck officer if Isidor might board a lifeboat with Ida. However, Isidor Straus flatly refused, telling Col. Gracie that he would not board before other men—not as long as there were women and children remaining.

He did entreat his beloved Ida to board lifeboat number eight, but when Ida realized that Isidor would not be joining her, she gave her fur coat to her maid, Ellen Bird, telling her she—Ida—would not be needing it.

Survivors later related Ida's now famous words to Isidor. They are often repeated as an example of unfailing love. I have many times observed the effect they have on our guests.

Ida's words to Isidor:

"As we were in life, so we shall be in death, together."

Ida and Isidor were last seen on the boat deck. Some say they were standing there, arm-in-arm. Others say they were sitting in deck chairs, holding hands. We can imagine this so vividly, a picture of what many of us would have felt when we realize that this is the sudden, frightening end. That would be especially meaningful when we are facing the end together with a companion we deeply love.

We live our lives with the understanding that someday there will be an end, even if we survive the many illnesses, accidents, disasters that are the normal threats to our fragile existence here upon a planet where weather turns savage, oceans assail our most technologically sound ships, and killer viruses resist our best medicines.

That is not to mention genetic flaws or the betrayals of our own biological bodies. Perhaps in the *Titanic* disaster we identify with these other humans who—though they were from another era, a time very different from our own—were nevertheless vulnerable human beings like us.

Isn't it true that in any era, no matter what the century, all of us have these universal similarities? These are the markers that make us human. And we identify with the sudden, shocking event that strips away so fiercely, with such immediacy, the protections we are so proud of.

The safest ship in the world, as they often referred to the *Titanic*, and—through stories of *Titanic* passengers—we are there. We feel the cold air, see the sharp, glittering stars flung across the night sky and experience the awful bump of realization that in a few moments we will be torn from the security and heady joy of experiencing the exultation of a marvelous creation of human ingenuity. And then, with horrifying suddenness, we are facing our unconscious fears, this understanding always somewhere deep within us, that someday death will take us.

And yet for us, and for our guests, there is a kind of victory that often brings tears, to see two people whose deep love overcomes all of this and that somehow there is victory through love. Though we feel the tragedy that Ida and Isidor will be frozen in that twenty-eight-degree water, we understand that the depth and genuineness of their love for one another proves that there is more.

Regardless of the disasters, illnesses, or biological weaknesses that must assail us, love does ultimately connect and empower us. It is a significant reason we identify with those who sailed the *Titanic*, as well as with all humans who have ever lived.

TITANIC MUSEUM ATTRACTION CREW

LAUREN ANDERSON

Lauren Anderson loves the family atmosphere at *Titanic Museum Attraction.* Because she is stationed in our retail shop, Lauren has daily opportunities to observe the enthusiasm of our guests.

"One of my favorite memories," she says, "is a family from Texas."

They had driven sixteen hours to Pigeon Forge and were so excited that they stopped at our museum before they even checked into their hotel.

"They were all big *Titaniacs.* Four generations of them," Lauren tells me. "They were exhausted from their trip, but so happy to be here. They had so much excitement going through the ship."

"The children said their favorite part was the twenty-six-foot-long, fifty-six-thousand-piece Lego ship in our Discovery Gallery. The ship was built by Brynyar Karl, a ten-year-old autistic boy from Iceland."

SAMANTHA BARNES

Samantha Barnes is a Crew Member who helps Admissions run smoothly. She smiles when she relates some of the more interesting comments she encounters as she welcomes guests to the museum.

"Not long after I started, a guest complemented the museum, stating that his favorite gallery was *Jackson Brown* gallery."

He must have been referring to the *Father Browne Photo Gallery*, which displays the only photographs of life onboard *Titanic.*

Samantha smiles as she remembers another guest.

"This guest asked me if Bob Hope was on the *Titanic.*"

The guest had heard that the famous comedian sailed on *Titanic's* maiden voyage.

One of Samantha's talents is her ability to subdue a rambunctious group of excited young guests with just one word: *Welcome.* She draws out the word so that it begins with a low croon which quickly escalates into an attention-grabbing command.

It must have a punch resembling what their teachers have trained them to respond to. The children immediately come to attention as the smiling Samantha begins her introductory remarks. They look somewhat dazed, as if wondering what just happened.

JANET BOYLE

Janet Boyle's opportunity to join our team at *Titanic Museum Attraction* began with one of those rare, life-changing phone calls. The call came as she was in the middle of her move from Florida to Tennessee.

"As I'm driving, I get a phone call asking me to come in for a job interview!"

Before deciding to move to Pigeon Forge, Janet would visit here. She was aware of our museum.

"I'd always been fascinated with the *Titanic,* and I decided that when I moved to Pigeon Forge, I would try to work at *Titanic Museum Attraction.* I applied, but what a thrill to get that call as I was driving here!"

Janet has been helping guests in the Gift Shop for nearly four years now, and—like so many of us—she is delighted with the exuberance of the children she encounters.

"They want to know everything about the *Titanic.* Many of them already know so much about the ship. They've been saving up their money. They've planned and looked forward to this. Some are here for their birthdays. For so many of our children, it's the most exciting experience they've ever had in their life."

Janet looks forward to interacting with each of our guests, but of course the children bring a special joy. We are swept up in their enthusiasm as we see through their eyes the excitement of what the *Titanic* meant to the world of 1912. And, of course, that excitement lifts and fascinates even now, more than a hundred years after the *Titanic* first thrilled and inspired the world.

STEPHANIE BUTTERS

Stephanie Butters, a talented actress, is very versatile at *Titanic Museum Attraction,* able to move seamlessly between Cast, Admissions, and Gift Shop.

She obtained a B.A. in Theater before joining *Titanic Museum Attraction.* During the summers, she pursues additional opportunities to extend her creative talents at *Sweet Fanny Adams Theatre* in Gatlinburg, where she performs with the talented cast there after her day at *Titanic Museum Attraction.*

Stephanie will never forget an encounter with a group from the New York area, and the connection she had with a woman in that tour group.

"I usually mention 9-11 in the Father Browne Gallery," she says. "The impact of that unthinkable terrorist attack was similar to how the *Titanic* disaster changed the world's perspective in 1912."

"A woman from the group pulled me aside and asked how much I remembered about 9-11. I told her that, being from New York myself, I remembered it clearly."

The woman told Stephanie that she had been on the thirty-seventh floor of the World Trade Center's Tower One that day, and she struggles even now to walk the surrounding streets. She still has nightmares.

"All I could do was hug her. It was chilling and very emotional to see a tragedy I remembered so well mirrored in my work at *Titanic Museum Attraction.*"

JOHN CANNEY

Often, we learn new details about *Titanic* passengers from visiting guests, and the information comes casually, even accidentally.

Titanic Museum Attraction Crew Members know that talented writer Jacques Futrelle and his wife, May, were First Class passengers on *Titanic's* maiden voyage. Futrelle was a talented fiction writer.

Crew Member John Canney, however, learned a fascinating footnote regarding the Futrelles as he chatted with a lady who asked him for a Jacques Futrelle boarding pass. John explained that we do not yet have a boarding pass for Jacques. However, he escorted the lady and her husband to our *Father Browne Photo Gallery* to show them our photograph of Jacques Futrelle.

The lady told John that her grandfather owned a garage in Scituate, Massachusetts, where Jacques and May Futrelle had built a house. Her grandfather would store their automobile for them during their occasional excursions to Europe.

Not long after the *Titanic* disaster, the garage owner and his wife received a postcard from May Futrelle advising them that Jacques had died in the *Titanic* disaster, and they would no longer have need of the car. Our guest advised John that she still has the postcard.

John is rather modest about his own background. But I have managed over the years to learn that he has been an actor for forty-five years. After studying Theater and Music in London, he was the comic lead in *Rose Marie* at London's Ashcroft Theater. He has also acted at Ford's Theater in Washington, D.C. and—as guest artist at Walter's State Community college—played Judge Turpin in *Sweeney Todd.*

Many thanks to veteran actor John Canney for uncovering this fascinating information about Jacques Futrelle and his wife, May.

DAVINA COPPLER

Davina Coppler handles virtually any position at the ship with poise and grace. Her portrayal of *Titanic* passenger Lucy, Lady Duff Gordon, however, has been particularly magical.

Davina says she will never forget an encounter with a young guest.

"I heard a little girl excitedly telling her mother what she liked about each of the Lady Duff Gordon dresses on display in the First Class Parlor Suite. As I swept into the room, the girl was expressing her desire to meet the designer."

"I introduced myself as Lucy, Lady Duff Gordon and thought the child was going to faint."

Davina learned that the girl was herself an aspiring young designer, and encouraged her to follow her dreams.

"Don't take no for an obstacle," I told her. "No obstacle is too great for those with a desire to succeed!"

Davina says that she herself has always been learning, stretching her abilities to see how far they'll go and what she can do next.

Management frequently relies on Davina to train and guide new employees, knowing they can trust her to convey the high standards with just the right blend of toughness, understanding, and support.

Davina is also a great cook and delights our Crew with the delicious confections she often leaves for us in the Galley.

ROY COUCH

Roy is a mechanical genius, and that's not an exaggeration. He just knows how to repair things.

When something mechanical stubbornly refuses to work, the response is immediate. We don't even have to think.

"Leave a note for Roy."

Or, if the problem occurs during Roy's shift, the response is, "Where's Roy? Someone find Roy."

We watch, mesmerized, as his deft fingers move with the precision of a trained surgeon. And there are many items behind the scenes at *Titanic Museum Attraction.* Roy keeps them working at their best.

But Roy also has a wonderful sense of humor. We cannot possibly be around Roy long before we are smiling, laughing at his comments. He has such a friendly, welcoming approach to life. Come what may, Roy usually embraces it good naturedly. We might be exasperated, but Roy shrugs and fixes it.

And guess who is the life of the party when we have our annual party or other special occasions? Well, there are several I could mention, but Roy is definitely one of them.

By the way, Roy is our Senior Maintenance Specialist. He's been with *Titanic Museum Attraction*, Pigeon Forge, nearly since the beginning.

BEVERLY DALTON

Affectionately known by our Crew Members as Little Bev, Beverly Dalton is a highly efficient Manager on Duty. I asked Bev for her thoughts about her experience behind the scenes at *Titanic Museum Attraction.* I was moved by what she told me.

"One of the things I do every single day is, when I get to that Grand Staircase, I always stop for just a minute and think about *Titanic*'s passengers and how we can keep their memory alive here at the museum."

Usually the opening manager each day, Bev likes the challenge.

"It's tough sometimes, but also very rewarding, especially when I see the children and the smiles on their faces."

COLE DEBERRY

Cole began as a Cast Member, but he has been a Manager on Duty since his promotion a few years ago. He told me that he will always remember an experience years ago when he portrayed Fireman John Podesta.

"A lady had four small boys with her. The boys were fascinated with me because I was so grimy."

The firemen worked in the Boiler Room, endlessly shoveling coal into furnaces set into three-story high boilers. Because firemen were sweaty and covered in coal dust and soot, they were known as the black gang, and these little boys were fascinated with Cole as John Podesta.

"I took them to our Boiler Room. We were shoveling coal, and they were so excited, though they were a little disappointed they weren't getting dirty. They couldn't understand why they couldn't look like me, but all four were grinning ear-to-ear."

Afterwards, the lady they'd come with pulled Cole aside.

"'What you don't know,'" she told me, "is that these boys are foster kids. The smallest of the four, we haven't seen him smile since we've had him. This is the first time we've ever seen him smile.'"

No doubt the boys, and that one smallest boy in particular, will always remember their encounter with Cole in his role as Fireman John Podesta.

JEREMY DUCHOW

Jeremy Duchow is said to have the entire *Titanic* schematic in his head. His fascination with the ship has led to a detailed knowledge of the ship's layout. We go to Jeremy when we have questions about *Titanic*'s schematics.

I observed Jeremy in action just the other day. In the Map Room, a guest holding the boarding pass for Assistant Surgeon John Simpson approached him.

Jeremy was portraying Fireman Joseph Dawson that day. He really looks the part—one of many soot-covered men who toiled in the boiler room shoveling coal endlessly into the furnaces. Jeremy keeps himself in top physical condition with workouts that include weight lifting. His massive shoulders and biceps give him the look of a strong, rangy Crew Member who has the stamina to sweat through ten hour shifts of shoveling coal into boiler room furnaces.

One guest approached Jeremy recently, holding out his boarding pass.

"I have a ship's surgeon," he said. "John Simpson. Where would his quarters be on the ship?"

Jeremy quickly led the man to the *Titanic* schematic in the Map Room and pointed to an area beneath the fourth smokestack.

"See this white area?" he asked. "That is the ship's hospital. John Simpson would work here, and his quarters would be near the hospital."

Jeremy went on to explain that a Crew Member's quarters would be located near his service area. And yes, on the *Titanic* we would nearly always use the masculine pronoun when referring to a Crew Member. Of the 913 Crew Members onboard *Titanic*, only twenty-three were women. It was still very much a man's world out at sea in 1912.

COURTNEY DUPONT

We talk *Titanic Museum Attraction*, and it is easy to focus on stories about our most visible Crew Members. But there are also *Titanic Museum Attraction* members working efficiently behind the scenes, such as Courtney Dupont. Courtney works closely with Carlos Orsi and Roy Couch to maintain high standards of cleanliness and order at our museum. Though our guests usually don't see them, it is their diligence that makes our museum glow.

For example, Courtney arrives every day before guests and often before our Crew Members. The duties are many and endless. But Courtney takes pride in her work. Nearly always quietly in the background, Courtney is constantly on the move in her daily quest to be certain that everything is splendid for our museum guests and—for that matter—for all of us.

Not only are guest facilities spotless, but facilities for crew are as well. We have our bathrooms and our galley where we relax on breaks. All of this requires regular work, and Courtney is always there from the beginning of each day, a constant presence.

She is part of the family. All Crew Members, no matter what our role, work together and give our best to make *Titanic Museum Attraction* a world-class museum that impresses and inspires our guests.

ELAINE FARONE

Ten years ago, Crew Member Elaine Farone and her family vacationed in the Pigeon Forge area, and that was it. They were hooked on our region and moved here.

Elaine is particularly delighted with the children she encounters on a daily basis as she works with guests in the Gift Shop. One small child in particular made her laugh.

"She was maybe five-years old and so serious as she explained to me that the *Titanic* wouldn't have broken apart when it hit the iceberg if it hadn't been built out of Legos."

We are constantly delighted with *Titanic* as seen through the perspective of a child.

RYAN FISCHER

Ryan Fischer is another of our Crew Members who has extensive background with acting: forty years in live theater.

But Ryan was bitten by the *Titanic* bug early on.

"I have been studying the *Titanic* since I was eight," he says.

And like me, he is captivated by the children who visit our museum.

"Not only do they ask exceedingly intelligent questions, but their responses can take us by surprise."

Ryan remembers one day when he was portraying Broadway theater producer Henry Harris.

"I was explaining that Henry Harris was a theater producer, and a boy raised his hand and asked me, 'What is a theater producer?'"

Ryan smiles as he relates his interaction with the boy.

"Do you know what I did?" Ryan-as-Henry Harris asked.

"Yeah," said the boy. "You *died* on *Titanic!*"

In addition to Henry Harris, Ryan portrays junior wireless operator Harold Bride and Third Class passenger John Kiernan. Ryan also looks great in a kilt when he appears as a Scottish officer.

LARRY FOSTER

Larry Foster, one of our M.O.D.'s (Managers on Duty), is an example of instantaneous creativeness. He can transition quickly into so many zany voices and characters for the Crew. He is my best example of this spontaneous creativeness that resonates through the Crew.

I believe this playfulness energizes all of us and migrates through us to our guests. We are, after all, creating a different world, helping them to feel this era that produced *Titanic.* This creative energy inspires us.

In his role as M.O.D. Larry exhibits a sense of calm and gentle authority as he addresses guests. He has a presence, so to speak, that conveys assurance and the certainty to guests that he will address their concerns immediately and effectively.

And his talent and experience in directing make Larry Foster the go-to man for producing performances that delight our guests, such as our annual Thanksgiving Day extravaganza.

JOHNNA GARRETT

Gift Shop Crew Member Johnna Garrett has always been drawn to the water. A long-time resident of Michigan before moving to East Tennessee, Johnna grew up on the water. She and her husband moved to the Smoky Mountains six years ago, and she loves her trips to the lake.

Johnna remembers a Gift Shop guest who had unusual plans for the Heart of the Ocean necklace she was purchasing.

"The lady told me she was planning on leaving her husband when she returned from vacation, which she'd already told him. As she paid for her Heart of the Ocean necklace, she told me she was going to leave it for him as a gift with a note: *My heart will go on without you.*"

There is apparently no end to the variety and creativity of our guests as they identify with the *Titanic* story and its many cycles of romance.

DENISE GRAY

As I've mentioned, our guests are the basis for *Titanic Museum Attraction.* As Crew, nearly every day includes a special memory or occasion which grows from interactions with our guests.

Denise Gray, who welcomes guests in Admissions, tells me she looks forward to one group each year.

"There is a 'special needs' group that visits our museum each year. Four years ago, one of the women gave me a beaded bracelet. I keep this bracelet in my locker, and I wear the bracelet each time they visit."

Denise says the woman hugs her and says she can't believe Denise still has the bracelet.

"She is so sweet. I would never have met her if I didn't work here."

Though Denise is most often in Admissions, she works in many different areas of the ship.

BRITTNEY GREEN

Brittney Green is another of the many Crew Members who credit opportunities at the museum for helping them discover and develop potential they never suspected was within them.

"When I was first hired in Admissions," she says, "I didn't know I would be doing speeches. It scared me at first because I had never given a public speech."

Today, however, museum guests would not suspect that Brittney ever had any reluctance to speak publicly.

One of Brittney's favorite parts of working in Admissions is the opportunity to meet people from all over the world.

"I love their enthusiasm," she says. "Even when there is a language barrier, I can tell they are excited to be here."

Brittney credits the supportive environment at *Titanic Museum Attraction* for giving her the confidence to develop a potential she hadn't known she possessed.

"It is the best job I've ever had," she says. "The Crew here is like a family to me, and I haven't felt that way anywhere else."

MISTY GREEN

Misty brings Polar to life for delighted children in our Interactive Gallery, where Tot Titanic features a flat-screen monitor that is a window into Polar, the *Titanic* bear. Misty is the voice of Polar.

Misty remembers so many encounters with guests who interact with Polar.

"One of my favorites was an Asian woman who just fell in love with Polar. She was jumping up and down saying how cute Polar is and how she'd love to take Polar home and love him always."

Misty also remembers a little boy who turned his back on Polar. Misty-as-Polar asked him, "Why do we have to be so quiet?"

The boy said, "Shhh. I don't want my dad to shoot you!"

The boy finally confided to Polar that his dad loves to hunt.

But the dad laughed and assured his little boy and the amused guests that he would never shoot Polar.

Misty says that portraying the voice of Polar for children is like *Candid Camera* and *Kids Say the Darndest Things* rolled into one.

NATHAN HEADRICK

Like Crew Member Jason McKeon, Nathan Headrick began as one of *Titanic Museum Attraction*'s youngest Crew Members. Hired on his eighteenth birthday, Nathan has never looked back, so to speak, and today he has been promoted to work with our IT (Information Technology) Specialist, Emily Densky.

"I just kept getting more and more opportunities to grow in the museum," Nathan told me. "I started as a Cast Member, learned how to work the Pavilion, greeting people and helping them enter the museum. Then I got to go deliver cookies to different businesses. I delivered comp tickets to the various Tennessee welcome centers."

Recently, IT Specialist Emily Densky was impressed with Nathan's ability to resolve various computer-related issues and recommended that he be promoted to her department.

As Nathan points out, though, everyone here has opportunities.

"At *Titanic Museum Attraction*, everyone who works here has this chance, the opportunity to keep growing. I love it."

JEREMY HILL

A member of our Admissions team, Jeremy is among the first Crew Members our guests encounter as they enter the museum. He enjoys the opportunity to interact with guests as he helps them begin their experience at *Titanic Museum Attraction.*

One guest encounter was especially meaningful to him on a personal level.

"I was able to interact with a breast cancer survivor during Breast Cancer Awareness month. It was a lady who arrived with her husband. She told me she was excited to be a breast cancer survivor, and she told me her story."

Jeremy presented the lady with the boarding pass for Lucille, Lady Duff Gordon, who lost her battle with breast cancer years after her voyage on *Titanic.*

"I shared with her how my own mother had recently passed away due to breast cancer. That lady's story reminded me of my mother, and I felt moved to share my own story with her. It helped me so much that she had shared her story with me."

JODI JUSTIS

Jodi Justis has quite a history with *Titanic Museum Attraction* Pigeon Forge. She was the very first Crew Member hired by owners John Joslyn and Mary Kellogg Joslyn.

Of course, Jodi has many memories, beginning with the *Titanic* Preview Center, a trailer which showcased the museum while it was under construction. Jodi smiles as she describes the day the hydraulic jacks failed and pitched the trailer at an angle.

"We heard *boom-boom-boom* and a whooshing sound as the trailer began to tilt. Construction workers had to use a forklift to straighten us out!"

Jodi says she will never forget the ten-year-old girl with MS (Multiple Sclerosis) who was determined to walk up the Grand Staircase.

"I put her wheelchair in the elevator, and her dad helped her up the stairs. She was so proud of herself for making it."

Jodi wears many hats at the museum. She works with our Educational School Sales division, connects with our sales clients for all of our special events. She is also the 'Key' Crew Member handling all of our ship social media.

DEBORAH MORRIS

Deborah, who works in our Gift Shop, fondly remembers the day she observed a woman who had no idea the man in line behind her was no other than John Joslyn, who—with his wife Mary Kellogg Joslyn—owns *Titanic Museum Attraction.*

"One day," Deborah told me, "John came into the Gift Shop as he sometimes does, to buy himself a snack. A lady in front of him had an extra coupon."

Deborah was amused when the lady in front of John turned to him and said, "Here, sir. Would you like this ten percent coupon? It'll save you a few cents."

John was surprised, but delighted.

"He could have received our twenty percent employee discount," Deborah told me, "but he was so thrilled the lady had given him a coupon."

Deborah shakes her head, remembering that day. "That woman didn't have a clue who he was, but I could tell that John was so touched and excited as he presented that ten percent coupon."

MATTHEW MOYER

Like Crew Member Jason McKeon, Matthew signed with *Titanic Museum Attraction* at the age of eighteen, and like Jason, Matthew loves interacting with museum guests, especially when he can be of special assistance.

Matthew remembers his encounter with a young lady whose physical challenge required her to use forearm crutches. He advised her group that they could either walk up the Grand or take the elevator to continue the second part of the tour upstairs.

Matthew was surprised when the girl began removing the metal wristbands and handed the crutches to her father, who looked concerned.

"Are you sure?" he asked.

She smiled and nodded, determined to have the experience of walking up the Grand Staircase. As most of our guests, she wanted through imagination to be there in that era, ascending the Grand Staircase.

The girl's father gently helped her to the first steps, but Officer Matthew stepped forward, offered his arm, and became her escort. Standing near her, tall and smiling, he patiently supported her so that she could enjoy the fullness of these moments.

The young girl returned the next day to thank Matthew and to let us know what a memorable experience this had been.

LESLEY NEWTON

Interesting to note connections between various Retail Shop Crew Members. One example is falling in love with the Great Smoky Mountain area and then deciding to move here. Lesley Newton is a case in point. She grew up in Florida and Georgia, but her father made it a family tradition to vacation in the Smoky Mountains.

Lesley's sister moved here to raise her family, and now Lesley is here. She has two sons, and one of them has joined her here. She loves to hike and camp. She and her son have a new passion to pursue together: birdwatching.

Lesley worked twenty-three years as a medical assistant. Her retail management experience includes Walmart, Kmart, and Target.

CARLOS ORSI

Titanic Museum Attraction Crew delight in our Maintenance Specialist, Carlos Orsi.

Originally from Argentina, Carlos speaks with a deep Spanish accent. Beyond his exotic pronunciation of English, though, is the culture he brings to us. Carlos is more like a favorite uncle to Crew Members.

For example, when one of the young ladies has a birthday, she will stand patiently, smiling, as Carlos lightly grasps her ears and gives them a tug for each of her years.

And there is also the high standard Carlos sets for working behind-the-scenes to make our ship literally glow. A tremendous amount of work is required to keep the museum beautiful, clean, and resplendent for our guests. Carlos works tirelessly, ceaselessly, and yet quietly. He makes it all seem so effortless.

Carlos recently received a huge honor. He was awarded Tennessee Employee of the Year. We are very proud, but not surprised. Carlos inspires us all with his positive attitude and amazing work ethic.

CLAIRE PALMER

Kate Winslet brought Rose to life on the big screen, and not long ago we issued a casting call, hoping to find a talented young lady to portray Rose at *Titanic Museum Attraction* to honor James Cameron's *Titanic.* We had costumes on display, and we were fortunate that Claire Palmer auditioned to portray Rose.

From the moment she became Rose at the museum, Claire immersed herself in the role. In her enthusiasm, though, she may have gotten carried away on at least one occasion. Here she relates one incident in her own words.

"I tried to recreate the party in Third Class scene with a Rose-obsessed little boy. When we started dancing and spinning in circles like they did in the movie, I accidentally lifted him off the ground. He had a great time, but I was horrified that I had just swung a little boy around the Music Gallery."

Well, as I said, Claire immerses herself in her roles with enthusiasm.

She is usually in our Music Gallery, because she is a talented musician. She plays the piano *and* the violin. Most recently, Claire portrays First Class passenger Marjorie Newell, a young violinist who later in life founded the New Jersey Symphony Orchestra.

JONATHAN PIERCE

When Jonathan is not filling in as an M.O.D., he portrays passengers such as Thomas Andrews, *Titanic*'s chief designer. Sometimes he is a First Class officer, helping our guests get started when they first arrive outside in the Pavilion, or welcoming them in Admissions.

Jonathan remembers scanning tickets one evening for a family of nine who had pre-purchased ten tickets.

"With tears in their eyes, they told me the tenth ticket was for their thirteen-year-old son, who had died just a day or two earlier. He had been looking forward to visiting *Titanic Museum Attraction.*"

Jonathan told the mother about how, on the night of the *Titanic* disaster, a woman noticed a crew member shivering in the water as he clung to the side of her lifeboat. She traded places with him throughout the night so that he would survive. In gratitude, he later presented her with his crew pin.

"That sounds like something my Conner would do," the mother said.

Jonathan removed his own crew pin.

"Ma'am," he said, "It would be my privilege to give you this so that we can honor your son as a Crew Member here this evening."

The mother grabbed Jonathan in a huge hug before attaching the pin to her daughter's sweatshirt, which bore Conner's name.

As the family entered the museum a few minutes later, the mother whispered to Jonathan, "I will never forget this moment."

CYNTHIA SIMPSON

Titanic Museum Attraction General Manager Cynthia Simpson brings shiploads of enthusiasm to the Crew through her effusive personality.

"I love my job," she says, and that is evident to all of us as she oversees the daily behind-the-scenes operations. Cynthia is a major force in helping the museum run smoothly and efficiently.

She began as an M.O.D. (Manager on Duty), and her ability to handle the challenges of management with a steady hand and a smiling disposition made her a top choice to step into the General Manager position when it opened several years ago.

Cynthia made it clear from the beginning that her door is always open. She even has a box in our Crew Galley with a label that reads, *Tell Cynthia all about it.* Her openness and genuine concern for our happiness is a large part of why she is much respected and appreciated in her capacity as General Manager of *Titanic Museum Attraction*, Pigeon Forge.

JESSICA SMITH

Because Jessica Smith works primarily in Receiving, processing merchandise for our Gift Shop, she rarely interacts with guests. Even so, she values the days when she is called to help in the Gift Shop and can interact with museum guests.

"One day—a rare day for me to be in the Gift Shop—I saw a man wearing an Army Vet hat and I told him THANK YOU! He pulled out his phone and showed me some pictures."

"The pictures were of a monument which was a life-size model of his son, who was killed in action in Iraq."

"I cried along with him, and I hugged him."

It is the people who visit our museum who remind us of our powerful connection to the *Titanic* disaster. We honor *Titanic* passengers and crew by telling their stories here at *Titanic Museum Attraction*. However, our own guests remind us of the ongoing connection we have with individuals who are so much like us who sailed on *Titanic*. In every era, there are families with hopes and dreams.

We see their excitement, but feel their sadness, too, when they have endured loss.

CHERYL SPANGERSBERG

Cheryl Spangersberg is a delightful Violet Jessop when she is not portraying First Class passenger Edith Rosenbaum.

Like so many of us, Cheryl especially enjoys the children who visit our museum.

"I especially enjoy our young *Titaniacs*, children who have learned so much about the *Titanic*. I love hearing what these children know. I have learned through their own stories of the *Titanic*."

Cheryl is a full-time Science teacher, and we see her during summers and school holidays. Whether she is a character or a First Class maid, she entices our guests with her clear, pleasant voice. No doubt her experience as teacher is responsible for her effectiveness in helping our guests learn about the *Titanic* and its historical period.

HEIDI SWANGEL

Gift Shop Crew Member Heidi Swangel enjoys the enthusiasm she encounters from families and how *Titanic Museum Attraction* allows for a celebration of life in all its variety.

"Our museum gives a place for guests and crew alike to share. I love interacting with our guests, and I love the many opportunities I have to make someone's day better."

Heidi has been particularly aware of how our Lego *Titanic* has inspired so many of our youngest guests and given them a platform for sharing their own creative projects and dreams. She remembers the enthusiasm of a young guest, Kole, who was excited about the Lego *Titanic.*

"His parents were so generous in sharing Kole's accomplishments, goals, and photos with me. I just love sharing the laughter and even the tears. Such a powerful experience."

BOB THONE

When I am portraying Father Francis Browne, I will often come into the Map Room as my shift begins to relieve Reverend Bateman, who is brought to life by Bob Thone, another of our crew members with an encyclopedic knowledge of *Titanic.*

Bob, as Reverend Bateman, will pretend to have a bone to pick, so to speak, with Father Browne. He amuses our guests by his way of showing the concern of a Protestant for a Catholic. Of course, Bob makes it into an opportunity for some harmless banter between us. Just another example of how we do enjoy the opportunity to interact with guests and feel energized by the creative atmosphere.

Bob has an insatiable appetite for *Titanic* scholarship. Constantly reading, his research has made him one of our go-to Crew Members for little- known details about the ship.

LAUREN TRASK

Lauren Trask is a very knowledgeable Crew Member. She amazes us with her encyclopedic knowledge of the *Titanic* passengers and crew, but also with her ability to portray so many of the passengers, including a precocious boy in Third Class, a young passenger named Frankie.

She often visits schools in the area, delighting elementary students with her portrayal of Frankie. Of course, Frankie was a little boy, and Lauren is a young woman. Often the school presentation will end with Lauren sweeping off Frankie's hat and allowing her long, blonde hair to cascade down her shoulders, surprising and delighting the students.

Lauren's other roles include her moving portrayal of Third Class passenger Leah Aks. And of course, she is often a First Class maid. There seems to be no end to Lauren's ability to bring to life a wide range of *Titanic* passengers for our guests.

SARAH TURNER

Sarah Turner is another talented Crew Member at *Titanic Museum Attraction.* She is quite versatile, helping as needed. She is also one of our crew members who visits area schools.

"I have been in love with *Titanic* since I was a little girl and still love learning and teaching people," she says.

Her fascination for *Titanic* led her to study history in college.

Sarah's other great love is dance. She minored in dance in college and is delighted for the opportunities at *Titanic Museum Attraction.*

"Through parade performances and annual Thanksgiving shows, I have the opportunity to dance. Never could I have dreamed I would find a position that involves history *and* dance."

One of Sarah's special memories is a *Titanic* New Year's party where she was chosen to play Belle from Disney's *Beauty and the Beast.*

"A little girl in *Hello Kitty* pajamas tugged on my dress and said, 'You look just like Belle.' "

"To her, I was a princess—something that even Disney couldn't give me."

Before joining us at *Titanic Museum Attraction* in Pigeon Forge, Sarah worked at Walt Disney World in Orlando, Fla., where she completed the Disney College Program.

BILL YOUNG

Bill enjoys bringing the story of the eight *Titanic* musicians, collectively known as the *Titanic* band, vividly to life for our guests.

For many, however, Bill is one of the highlights of their entire tour through the museum because of the music he coaxes from his vintage violin, "Vin." A professional musician, Bill has entertained audiences in venues across the region for decades.

In Bill's trained hands, Vin reverberates with rich, deep tones that hold our guests captive. Guests linger in the Music Gallery just to experience Bill's unique sense of humor and music worthy of *Titanic* band leader Wallace Hartley or John Law Hume. Both specialized in the violin.

Bill also plays the beautiful Ivers & Pond grand piano that dominates the Music Gallery. Built in 1906, it is from the same era as *Titanic*. Guests often remark on the beautiful tone of this piano as Bill, or one of our guests, plays.

Needless to say, Bill Young—our Officer Bill—maintains standards of excellence associated with the talented *Titanic* band and, of course, with our own world-class *Titanic Museum Attraction.*

Photos

Me as Col. Archibald Gracie posing with Laura and Sarah Jennings, great granddaughters of George Kemish, *Titanic* fireman. Completing the photo is Cynthia Simpson, *Titanic Museum Attraction* General Manager, and Officer Craig Johnson, *Titanic Museum Attraction* Crew Member on the day Craig and I gave these descendants a V.I.P. tour of the museum.

First Class maid Lauren Trask with her trusty nail clippers.

Crew Member Jason McKeon clowning around with me as Father Francis Browne, the Jesuit Priest who captured the only photographs we know of that show life onboard *Titanic*.

Scheduled to be on display at *Titanic Museum* Attraction in 2020, the Wallace Hartley violin brought $1.7 million at auction in 2013. That is more than any other *Titanic* artifact.

Enjoying a moment with Brynjar Karl on Scotland Road, the behind-the-scenes area for our *Titanic Museum Attraction* crew members. Brynjar was ten years old when he built his 56-thousand-piece Lego *Titanic*. During his visit to *Titanic Museum Attraction*, Pigeon Forge in the Spring of 2018, he is a handsome, outgoing sixteen-year old.

Brynjar's 56-thousand-piece, 26-foot-long Lego *Titanic* on display in the Discovery Gallery. Brynjar, who has autism, built his ship in only eleven months.

Notes

Notes

Notes

53685187R00085

Made in the USA
Columbia, SC
20 March 2019